Your After-Credits Scene

A Nerd's Guide to Wills,
Trusts, and Legacy

M. Cecilia Amo

Your After-Credits Scene: A Nerd's Guide to Wills, Trusts, and Legacy

Scripture quotations are taken from the Holy Bible, New Living Translation, copyright © 1996, 2004, 2015 by Tyndale House Foundation. Used by permission of Tyndale House Publishers, Carol Stream, Illinois 60188. All rights reserved.

Cover Illustration by Ruben
Cover Design by Peaceful Profits

Paperback ISBN:
978-1-967587-32-2

ePub ISBN:
978-1-967587-33-9

To everyone who's ever been told their passions didn't matter—your wonder, your dreams, and the ones you love most are the very legacy worth protecting.

Table of Contents

Table of Contents

Rewriting the Script on Estate Planning

You'd think it'd be like a game show,
but think of a community theatre
production of a tax return.

–Benoit Blanc, *Knives Out*

E veryone knows that when someone wealthy passes away, the family lawyer gathers the family around a beautiful mahogany table in a cozy, book-lined room for the reading of the will. Or is that really how it works? What's fact and what's fiction when it comes to estate planning? That's exactly what this book is about.

We've all seen this dramatic scene dozens of times: a grieving family listens with bated breath as the family lawyer pulls a packet of papers from a heavy leather briefcase and then reads the will. If you've seen the film *Knives Out*, you know exactly what I'm referring to. Shortly after Harlan Thrombey, the wealthy head of the family, is found dead, we see the family sitting in a loose semi-circle in a richly decorated room (complete with mahogany furniture) around Alan Stevens, the family lawyer, who breaks down Harlan's assets.

When Alan informs the family that Thrombey recently changed his will and left everything to his personal nurse, Marta Cabrera, the family leaps from their chairs, yelling that they will contest the will. The chaos that ensues supports what Benoit Blanc (one of the private investigators who is trying to uncover what happened to Thrombey) says about will readings: they really are like a tax return performed by a community theater.

Dramatic will readings like this make a great framework for mystery movies, but they are far from what happens in real life.

Unfortunately, what we see on TV and in movies often shapes our understanding of everything, especially the law. From films like *Knives Out*, the courtroom drama of *Law & Order*, the madcap antics of *Boston Legal*, and the sharp-tongued legal maneuvering of Mike and Harvey in *Suits*, popular entertainment makes us feel like we're learning insider secrets with every episode. But what makes for thrilling prime time TV and feature films rarely reflects reality.

The truth is that most of us don't have the legal expertise to discern what's real and what's just good storytelling. While we know that we can't take the stand in the courtroom in our own defense and yell, "You can't handle the truth!" at the prosecutor, we might not be so discerning when it comes to less well-known aspects of the law, like estate planning.

But here's the thing: estate planning is just as significant as other legal issues people face. Sure, it's not as dramatic as a murder trial or an embezzlement case, but how often are you planning to be put on trial for those types of things? Don't answer that. I'm not your attorney (at least not yet).

Estate planning is one of the most important yet overlooked steps you can take for your family's future. It ensures that everything and everyone you love will be cared for in the event of your death or incapacity. It's about intentional living, protecting loved ones, and building a meaningful legacy— regardless of marital status, parenthood, or wealth.

Yes, a will is a fine document, and everyone should have one. But on its own, it's just not enough. It overlooks the countless threads that make up your life: your family, assets, values, and legacy.

There's so much more at stake than just money. Do you really want to trust everything you have and the legacy you'll leave behind to what you've learned on TV?

Why I Wrote This Book

What comes to mind when I say the word *estate*? Do you envision large Regency-period mansions, as portrayed in *Bridgerton*, or the rolling green hills surrounding *Downton Abbey*? Or perhaps you picture something more modern, like a luxury apartment on New York's Millionaires' Row or a beachside mansion in Miami, complete with a superyacht moored to the back dock.

In some sense, those assumptions are correct. Sure, the word "estate" can refer to sprawling properties or large investment portfolios. But really, it's just a fancy legal term that refers to everything you own. That's it. We all have estates. Your estate includes things like the house you own or that savings account you've been quietly building, but it also includes all the little things too: photos of your loved ones on your phone, that old Star Wars drinking glass that's been with you since you were a kid, or that rare Pokémon card you got by chance. These aren't just possessions; they are part of your estate, and they make up the story of your life.

It doesn't matter how much or how little you have. If you own *anything*, you have an estate. And if you want to ensure that your belongings and the people you love are taken care of, you need a plan.

That's where I come in.

Not only as an attorney, but also as someone who understands that behind every legal document is a human story worth protecting. I'm writing this book because I believe estate planning should feel more like wrapping your family in a warm embrace than drowning them in legal jargon.

I'm writing this book to share what you need to know about estate planning to make the process a little less scary and maybe even allow you to have a bit of fun along the way. Because the alternative to not having a plan? It's like leaving your family to navigate a maze full of danger while blindfolded and heartbroken.

During the hardest part of their lives—when they are actively grieving the loss of you—your family won't have access to your savings, real estate, or personal property because it will be tied up as the state tries to sort out everything you own. But I'm here to help make sure your family won't face such hardships or have to struggle through your loss on their own.

While those DIY will planners may seem like a tempting alternative, they aren't legally binding and can easily become outdated. (More on that later!) DIY planning, and to some extent traditional estate planning, focuses on the "what" (a set of documents that look official and seem complete) but misses the "why" behind each decision. Sure, you'll get a stack of documents that might make you feel accomplished, as if you've checked an important box off your endless to-do list. But without understanding the purpose of each decision, your family might face unnecessary complications.

The reality is that a stack of papers that you stick in a drawer and never look at again is not a real plan.

Here's a lesson I've learned after years of practice: when you understand the "why" behind the planning, the "how" becomes much clearer.

Before we go any further, let me tell you about myself and why I care so much about helping you protect your legacy.

My Origin Story

I decided I wanted to be a lawyer when I was 5 years old, right after my grandfather died. He had been my primary caretaker, and even though I didn't really know what a lawyer did, I knew that's what he was. In my 5-year-old brain, that was enough; I was going to be a lawyer too.

Fortunately, it all worked out, and I loved learning about the law. Honestly, I look back at studying for the bar exam as one of the best times of my life. (Which probably tells you a lot about my personality.)

When I first began practicing law, my vision of what it meant to be a lawyer was undoubtedly influenced by media portrayals of lawyers. I thought I had to be an aggressive, no-nonsense lawyer in a sharp gray or navy suit who could glare a witness into admitting the truth, just like Lara Flynn Boyle's character on *The Practice*.

The truth is, I'm not intimidating. I'm a five-foot-tall Asian woman, and when I passed the bar, I looked so young that some people thought I was still in high school. While I've come to embrace the fact that my strength doesn't come from being fearsome but from being approachable, I initially resisted that reality. I thought the only way people would take me seriously was if I came across as tough and unapproachable, as if I had to wear this big, intimidating "lawyer" cosplay costume.

And, for a while, I did wear it.

When I was hired at The Cochran Firm (the firm that represented O.J. Simpson) in Los Angeles, California, I became the first Asian American attorney they'd ever brought on. That moment carried weight, especially within the Filipino-American community. I was featured in newspapers, interviewed on *Balitang America*, invited to be a guest panelist on the *SpeakOut* talk show on The Filipino Channel, and the firm even bought ad space in Filipino-American media to highlight the milestone. I joined the board of the Philippine

American Bar Association of Los Angeles, and I was known as "that Filipina attorney at The Cochran Firm."

It was an incredible honor. But it also came with pressure. I felt like I had to represent something bigger than myself. Like I was supposed to represent success, professionalism, and pride for an entire community. There wasn't room to be unsure, awkward, or even human. I was supposed to be polished. Impressive. Unshakable. So I kept trying to perform according to the version of "lawyer" I thought everyone expected.

What people didn't see was how out of place I felt. I was homeschooled as a child, deeply nerdy, and socially out of step. I was also quite introverted (and possibly even a little ADHD, though I didn't have a name for it back then). I just didn't know how to relate to the other associates during the usual office small talk. It felt pointless and exhausting. The other associates seemed to speak a language I hadn't learned yet, and I felt like I was on the outside as everyone else bonded over things I didn't know how to engage with.

There were moments that stayed with me. Like walking into the break room and sensing a shift in the energy. Conversations would stop, glances would pass, and no one would explain what I'd just walked into. One time, someone even said, "Don't you hate it when the person you were just talking about walks in?" loud enough for me to hear. Whether or not it was meant for me, I felt it. I got the message.

Looking back, it was like I was a character in *Mean Girls*, but instead of wearing pink on Wednesdays and writing a slam book, we wore boring suits and wrote motions.

The more I tried to perform that version of "lawyer," the more I felt like I was drifting further from who I really was and who I wanted to be.

Eventually, I stopped trying to impress people who didn't really see me. I learned (sometimes painfully) that trying to be someone I'm not just doesn't work.

That authentic me—that's the version you're hearing from now.

I'm someone who knows that connection matters more than performance. I'm not trying to dominate the room. I'm looking around the room for the people who feel overlooked.

My strength has always been in making people feel safe enough to open up. I have this instinct inside me; I'm always drawn to the person in the room that no one else is paying attention to. I want to make space for them. I want to hear *their* story.

That instinct to create space, to listen, and to help people feel safe eventually reshaped the way I practiced law.

I spent years representing plaintiffs in catastrophic injury and wrongful death cases, fighting hard for families going through the worst moments of their lives. But I realized I didn't want to just show up after the crisis. I wanted to help people plan ahead, so that if and when something did go wrong, things could go as smoothly as possible for the people they love.

For the past several years, I've focused exclusively on helping individuals and families create thoughtful, heart-centered plans that reflect their real lives, not just their assets. I founded AMO LAW Legacy Planning[1] to provide a space where

---

1 www.amo-law.com.

people could have honest conversations about life, death, and everything in between, ultimately creating a plan that gives them clarity and peace of mind.

Of course, I didn't always understand how important that kind of safety was until life handed me a few lessons I never saw coming.

Creating My Own Safe Space

When I was a kid, my family was Catholic, but we felt pretty disconnected from the church. By the time I reached high school, my mom had started looking for some sort of spiritual connection for our family. She eventually found a Christian church that sounded ideal; they said we would have a more personal relationship with God than the Catholic church allowed, so we joined.

And suddenly, there I was, a very socially awkward, homeschooled teen with overprotective parents, attending Sunday school and interacting with people my own age for what felt like the first time in my life. Eventually, I started liking a guy, and we'd sit next to each other at Sunday school. Immediately after the first time we sat together, the entire church gossiped about it and made it sound horrible, like he was going to corrupt me. They convinced my parents that I shouldn't be allowed to see him, but of course, I snuck out to see him anyway.

Long story short, I was in a serious car accident while driving home from his place one night and landed in the hospital. The next morning, I was lying in my hospital bed, on superstrong pain meds, and everything hurt. Because I told them I was on my way home from my boyfriend's house when I got into the accident, my parents brought in our pastor, who essentially asked me to confess all of my sins in front of them.

It was the most humiliating experience of my young life. When our pastor decided to hold a group prayer right there in my hospital room, all I could think was, "This is wrong. This is awful. I'm never going to church again." The church is supposed to be a welcoming and loving community, the exact opposite of what I experienced that day.

Ten years later, when my sister convinced me to go to her church, I went in cosplay, complete with colored contacts and a wig. I figured if they were going to judge me, they might as well do it the moment I walked through the door. But no one batted an eye. They treated me like any other person walking through the door. For the first time in a long time, I actually felt safe in a church. So I stayed. Eventually, I was baptized and (because I'm me), I started Jesus Otaku, an anime outreach ministry, in 2012 (back when most people still thought all anime was basically porn).[2]

I'm a nerd at heart. I love fandom, and it's the easiest way I know to explain things. One reason nerd culture is so great is that it is both diverse and accepting. Nerd culture became a lifeline for me after I left that first church. Like so many others, I felt like I didn't belong in other environments and wasn't welcome in a space that was supposed to be inclusive. Comic-Con and anime conventions, on the other hand, were

---

2 www.jesusotaku.com.

welcoming and provided a space that enabled me to step out of the suit-and-script version of "lawyer" I thought I had to play so that I could finally start showing up as myself.

Nerd culture welcomes everyone. (Sure, there may be a few gatekeeping jerks who'll demand that you prove that you didn't "get into it because of the movie" and that you've been a fan since before it was cool, but they are far from the norm!) I especially love fandom conventions. Anime conventions and comic conventions were the first places where I found a real community.

There are many people like me who feel like outsiders, have been hurt by their church, or just want to connect to something spiritually. I realized that I had to share that welcoming spirit with my fellow nerds in fandom spaces, so I founded Jesus Otaku. We cosplay, talk about manga and anime, and attend anime conventions where we remind people that God loves them just the way they are.

In 2020, I met my mentor, Ali Katz, and became a member of the Personal Family Lawyer® network.[3] It's a wonderful community of heart-centered, holistic lawyers who welcomed my nerdy self into the group and even advocated for my authenticity.

These experiences are what led me to start my own practice and brought me to a point in my life where I no longer have to compartmentalize who I am to be accepted by exclusive communities. I can be a lawyer, a nerd, and a Christian all

---

3 www.personalfamilylawyer.com

at the same time, and I want others to experience that same feeling of overall safety.

The next time you're at the L.A. Comic Con, come find me! I usually have a booth in the exhibit hall. Tell me what your favorite fandom is, even if I haven't heard of it yet. I love listening to people talk about what they're passionate about. But be warned! I'm definitely going to tell you about my passions as well. I hope you like Star Wars, Harry Potter, and anime!

Oh, and remember that boy from Sunday school that my parents thought would corrupt me? I married him.

All of this—my journey through law, my love of community, my passion for helping people through difficult times—brings me to the work I do every day: estate planning. Looking back, I realize every chapter of my story was teaching me that life's most important moments aren't just about what happens to us, but about how we prepare for what happens next.

You know what's fascinating? Some of the most critically acclaimed Star Wars stories in recent years, such as *Rogue One* and *Andor*, aren't about flashy lightsaber battles or Force powers. They're about the quiet heroes who understand that preparation makes all the difference. Every sacrifice, every small act of rebellion, and every careful plan builds toward that one crucial moment when Princess Leia receives the Death Star plans. Those characters know they might not see the victory, but they make sure those who come after them have everything they need to succeed.

From helping people rebuild after their worst days to witnessing the profound peace that comes from proactive planning, I've learned that the most powerful thing you can do for your family isn't just telling them you love them—it's showing them by making sure they're protected, no matter what the future holds.

Unfortunately, many people believe that simply writing down what they want will cover it all. They don't realize that estate planning involves far more than that.

When Good Intentions Meet Legal Reality

Essentially, estate planning is a fancy term for making a plan for what happens to your stuff and the people you care about in the event of your death or incapacity.

When the topic of estate planning arises, most people think about what happens after someone dies. But they don't think about what happens when someone is incapacitated. Who's going to pay the bills, take care of the kids, and make sure your furry, feathered, or scaled family members are properly cared for?

Let's consider what could happen outside of the hospital room. It's comforting to assume that someone will step in to pay the bills or take care of your kids and pets if something happens to you. You have close friends or family who'd do that for you, right? But will they have access to your bank accounts? Do they even know which bills need to be paid? Can they make personal health choices for you or your children?

Now here's an even scarier thought: what if the person who *does* step in isn't the one you'd want? Maybe you'd choose your best friend to care for your kids, but your mother insists she has the legal right to do so. But let's say your mother doesn't share your religious or political values. Let's say her values are the polar opposite of yours. What might your children experience under her care?

Think about it like this: how different would Harry Potter's life have been if Sirius Black, Remus Lupin, or even Hagrid had taken him in instead of Aunt Petunia? Sure, in the wizarding world, a blood relative was required to protect him. However, in the real world, there's no such magic, only the legal groundwork you prepare in advance. But don't worry; I'm here to simplify the process and ensure that your children will be cared for exactly as you want them to be.

Before you tell me you've organized all of your important documents in something like a Nokbox that bills itself as a "next of kin box"[4] or bought one of those end-of-life planning books on Amazon with charmingly morbid titles like, *Sorry, It's Your Problem Now* and *I'm Dead, Now What?*, let me ask this: how legally binding are they?

The answer? Not at all.

While those are a great way of recording your wishes and organizing important information, a court won't recognize them as valid legal documents.

These tools may have fill-in-the-blank sections for important details, but they can't ask you questions about things you

---

4 www.thenokbox.com.

haven't even considered yet. When your family has questions and needs guidance after you're gone, a book filled with your notes won't help them navigate the complex decisions they'll face when emotions are high and time is short.

You need someone who can hold space for these difficult conversations—a trusted advisor who can ask the right questions to help you consider what really matters and ensure that your wishes are clear, comprehensive, and legally enforceable.

While an estate plan won't help or prevent incapacity, it's a way to maintain control during a time when you will have no control over important things. Essentially, you're making choices now so that someone doesn't have to make them for you later. It will ensure that all of the people and things you are responsible for are cared for by someone else until you get back home.

Estate planning is something you do for yourself (especially for situations where you may become incapacitated), but really, it's a huge act of love. I like to say that it's the weirdest and most misunderstood love language.

It's also what will guarantee that your assets (your retirement, life insurance, and savings), along with your possessions (like the anime figure collection you keep in the paid, air-conditioned storage unit), go to the right people.

The other option is to let the government decide how your assets and possessions will be distributed. Probate, the state's "default plan," will tie your assets up in court for months to years, depending on the complexities of your estate. Not only does that mean your family won't have access to the funds when they need the money to take care of bills, but it also means that whatever money is in the estate will be drained by legal fees.

When your assets are overlooked (a fancy way of saying that there's no one to claim them), they'll go into the Department of Unclaimed Property (think of the Room of Hidden Things in the Harry Potter series) or into probate (which varies by state in the US). If there's no one to legally claim your assets, the government can take them. Essentially, probate is a lawsuit against your family during what is likely the hardest time of their lives.

I don't know about you, but I've never been a fan of default settings. When I'm playing a video game, I want to adjust the sound and lighting, and enable the invert Y-axis option in the camera settings (so that my camera points to where I want it to go). Sometimes, I'll spend hours customizing my character so it reflects the version of me that I want to experience while playing the game. Many of us have even spent money on customized skins for our characters, weapons, and armor because we don't want to look like everyone else when we log into *Call of Duty* or *World of Warcraft*.

If you're willing to invest time and money customizing a video game character's appearance, why would you accept the state's generic, one-size-fits-*none* default plan for something infinitely more important? Namely, the protection and care of everything and everyone you love most.

Before We Begin: What to Expect from This Book

As we journey through the different landscapes of estate planning together, you'll notice that I've woven specific family scenarios into some of the chapters. You'll find chapters for parents with young children, complex families with their own set of dynamics, and even unmarried or childfree people who've often been told they "don't need estate planning." (Spoiler alert: that's absolutely not true.)

But every chapter is written for you, regardless of which category resonates with your current life. It's kind of like the interconnected stories in the Marvel Cinematic Universe (MCU). Even if you're not particularly invested in Scott Lang's journey as Ant-Man, understanding his story becomes crucial when you need to appreciate how the Quantum Realm saves everyone in *Endgame*. Each family scenario I share reveals different layers of estate planning that could touch your life and the lives of the people you love in ways you might not expect.

I encourage you to read through each scenario; you might be surprised by what resonates with you. Every scenario we'll explore is really about the same fundamental human truth: we all want to protect the people who matter most to us.

Your Roadmap to Legacy

Just like any great adventure, you need to know where you're headed before you begin. You wouldn't start a road trip to Comic-Con without checking out hotel options, scoping out the best food spots, and marking the must-see panels on your schedule, right?

This book is your guide to estate planning. I'll show you the best destinations and help you avoid the places that'll leave you exhausted and discouraged. We'll start by exploring what holistic estate planning actually means, then bust the myths that keep people stuck at the starting line. From there, we'll dive into real scenarios that show how the right planning protects your family while the wrong approach (or no approach) can create chaos.

Whether you're safeguarding your children from ending up with Aunt Petunia, navigating complex family dynamics, planning for your chosen family, or protecting that prized collection you've spent years building—we'll cover it all. And because I care about your journey, I'll also help you understand the risks associated with DIY plans and help you choose the right attorney for your unique needs.

Ready for Your Legacy Adventure?

Just like that trusty lightsaber or magical artifact in your favorite stories, a well-crafted estate plan becomes your tool to ensure that, when the time comes, your legacy endures exactly as you intended.

So grab your favorite drink, find a comfy spot, and let's explore how love becomes a legacy through thoughtful estate planning. Because your story matters, and the people you care about matter.

Come with me if you want to…well, if you want your legacy to live on long after you become one with the Force.

Chapter 1

Not Your Parents' Estate Plan—
How Holistic Estate Planning Can
Help You Leave a Legacy that
Actually Reflects Who You Are

---

*When do we get to stop reacting to our parents and
start living for ourselves?*

–Tali, *Mass Effect 3*

When I started writing this book, many people asked me the same question: why are you telling millennials and Gen Xers about estate planning? Aren't they too young for that? Estate planning is for retirees and grandparents, not people in the prime of their lives.

What's more, these people often tell me that their parents and grandparents didn't even need an estate plan because they had a will. But they don't realize that the world our parents and grandparents lived in was fundamentally different from ours. Their estate planning strategies were designed for a simpler time when assets were primarily physical. You could walk into a bank with a death certificate and access an account. "Property" didn't include NFTs (non-fungible tokens) or domain names. They typically chose the cheapest or easiest option—the free will template, the lowest-cost attorney, or whatever else got the job done for the least amount of money. In that simpler time, they might have been able to do that without many consequences. However, over the past few decades, laws changed, regulations multiplied, and tax codes became more complex.

It's not just about legal complexities; our values are inherently different now because of how our world has changed. Not only are we the first generation to have to plan for our digital lives, but we also focus on things that will make our lives better now rather than waiting until we retire to "live the good life." In fact, 63% of Gen Z and 59% of millennials would rather spend money on life experiences like travel and concerts.[5] Since 1987, this experience spending has increased by 70%.[6] Gen X spends the most money annually in general, averaging over $83,000, but they're also seeking a balance between quality and price, valuing products that cater to their specific needs.[7]

Simultaneously our lives have also become increasingly complex. The growing acceptance of nontraditional family structures; the rise of grind culture (where many of us have

---

5 Serah Lewis, "Roughly 60% of Millennials, Gen Z Would Rather Spend Money on 'Life Experiences' Like Traveling, Concerts Now Than Save for Retirement—Are They Making a Big Mistake?" Yahoo! Finance, December 1, 2023, https://finance.yahoo.com/news/roughly-60-millennials-gen-z-110000580.html?guccounter=1&guce_referrer=aHR0cHM6Ly9kb2NzLmdvb2dsZS5jb20v&guce_referrer_sig=AQAAACePp85K-RhVOoaxrDAUsjZA6TJGkepSgOsWB1jlUuN3_qLKT_JyeKBAMybuwholTnhBekJ8EHr0Q3mOScyzI9BZ0NL-rYkX5CZRcvard2F77k3nG37lw146wVU5ER5sE6G7G4Ya3Plo_XQxj02cYYSqSiDaBM7wdoJp4uZhW-c5.

6 Saiidi Uptin, "Millennials Are Prioritizing 'Experiences' Over Stuff," CNBC, May 6, 2016, https://www.cnbc.com/2016/05/05/millennials-are-prioritizing-experiences-over-stuff.html.

7 Preethi Lodha, "Here's How Different Generations in the US Spend Their Income," World Economic Forum, October 5, 2022, https://www.weforum.org/stories/2022/10/americans-spend-their-money-by-generation/.

second jobs, side hustles, and small businesses); and the rollercoaster fluctuations of the economy and housing market over the last five decades have all changed the nature of estate planning.

However, we're so deeply embedded in the wildly complex time we live in that we don't recognize how different our lives are from those of our parents and grandparents. Just like Jim Carrey's character in *The Truman Show* went about his day unaware of the cameras filming his every move, these updated considerations feel normal until someone points them out. The assumptions that guided older generations simply won't work for us, which means it's time to rewrite our understanding of estate planning and recognize how important it truly is.

Why You?

Traditional estate planning is based on a set of assumptions. The first is that it's for people who are about to die. But that assumption hinges on the belief that creating an estate plan means that you're planning for your death, when in fact, you're planning for the people who will live on after you're gone.

All of those things you have to live for—your partner(s), children, friends, pets, and charitable causes you champion— will need to be taken care of when you're gone. If something happens that incapacitates you, your family will need to make decisions regarding your care. Accidents can happen at any time, and the Grim Reaper will eventually come for us all. Sadly, unlike in the life-simulation game *The Sims*, your family can't bargain with Grim to keep you around longer.

People also asked why I was writing this specifically for nerds rather than for everyone between 30 and 60 years old. On one level, this book is for everyone. Everyone who has stuff and people they love needs an estate plan. But on a deeper, more meaningful level, I'm writing this for you, my fellow nerds, because no one is speaking to us about this important topic.

We're all too familiar with people not speaking to us and that visceral feeling of not being welcomed at the table—and trust me, I know that feeling firsthand. But as adults, we've made our own tables and surrounded ourselves with people who are as unique as we are. We're proud to be different and to challenge the status quo.

We cosplay, talk about the fandoms we're part of, curate our shelves like museum exhibits, dye our hair vibrant colors, and play Dungeons & Dragons in public spaces. We unapologetically attend Comic-Con, Dragon Con, and every other fandom con in between. We're at a point in our lives where we no longer try to conform to what society at large says we should be.

The countless estate planning guides available on Amazon were written for the most generic audience imaginable. None of them were written for us, nor do they address our specific needs or the perspectives we value.

To be honest, many read so much like textbooks that I'm surprised they don't include quizzes at the end or links to online exams. They're dry and boring. Even more concerning is that many of them try to show you how to DIY your estate plan (which, as you'll find out in Chapter 7, rarely works in your favor regardless of how many books you read).

The point of this book isn't to show you how to create an estate plan; it's to demonstrate why you need to work with an experienced, relational estate planning attorney who will ask the right questions, help you craft a holistic Life & Legacy Plan, and ensure that your plan adapts to your life throughout the years to come. It's meant to show you some of the challenges you'll face without a plan and explain why you don't want to use a one-size-fits-all approach, or even worse, go at it alone.

So, What IS an Estate Plan, Anyway?

Although I've spent a lot of time discussing why you need an estate plan, you're probably thinking, "If it's not just a will, what *is* an estate plan, anyway?"

Estate planning is a proactive plan you make about what happens to you in the case of your incapacity. It also details what happens to your loved ones and your assets when you die. It's legally enforceable, allowing you to state your wishes and have them honored.

But beyond typical estate planning documents, there are also life and legacy planning aspects like an ethical will, which pertains to the values and intangible plans that are worth considering. Once you've made these choices and made them legally enforceable, you can live more fully and with less anxiety, knowing you've done everything possible to protect the people who matter most to you.

Estate planning is not only about *what* you own, but also about *how* you own it. Let's say you own a house. Is it jointly owned with a spouse, partner, family member, or friend? Has a beneficiary been designated? This is more than just choosing someone in your own mind because designating them is officially identifying them in legal paperwork. These details may seem small, but they carry big legal consequences. The way something is owned can completely change how it's handled in your plan, which is why no two plans look exactly alike (or at least, they shouldn't).

Estate planning is how you opt out of your state's default one-size-fits-*none* system. It gives you the power to decide what happens, how it happens, and who's in charge—before someone else does. Ask yourself: do I want oversight of my assets, or do I want a court making those decisions for me, like the Ministry of Magic controlling Harry Potter's fate?

The state already has a plan for you. But as I mentioned in the Introduction, it's essentially a lawsuit filed against your family for the benefit of your creditors and the government, which is paid for with your own money. No one wants to be remembered as someone who didn't plan to keep their loved ones out of court.

I've brought up probate multiple times throughout this chapter, and you're probably wondering, "What is probate and why is it so bad?" Well, let's get into that.

Probate: The Default Plan You Don't Want

Probate is the state's default plan that kicks in when someone dies with or without a will. One of the biggest misconceptions about wills is that having one means your family can skip probate. In reality, a will doesn't avoid probate at all. Probate is the court process required to validate the will, appoint the executor, and oversee the distribution of assets. This process can be lengthy, costly, and public, even when there are no disputes.

Probate is how the legal system decides what will happen to your debts and assets (cars, houses, money, and property) and decides who gets what. Retirement accounts, insurance policies, and assets that are jointly owned or have a designated beneficiary who is identified may not go to probate. (However, you do want to make sure the right people are listed as beneficiaries to your retirement and insurance. You don't want to make the mistake of leaving your ex as the beneficiary of your million-dollar retirement account.)

Regrettably, some people try to rely only on beneficiary designations because it seems "simpler" than having an estate plan. In reality, that approach becomes complicated very quickly, and it leaves no room for contingency planning if life doesn't go exactly as expected. Plus, it cannot go into effect in the event of your incapacity. If you have an executor (a person named by your will to carry out the dispensation of your estate), they will handle most of this process. Note that even with an executor, estates can take up to a year or more to be settled.

If you don't have a will (which typically names an executor), the courts will designate someone (called an administrator) to locate your loved ones and relatives and sort out your assets. Not only does that mean your loved ones won't have access to your estate for an extended period, but also means that money from your estate will be used to pay the courts for their services. And if there is a conflict over your estate, then things will get even more expensive. There will be filing fees, administrator fees, accounting fees, attorney fees, and other court-related expenses, which will all be paid for by your estate. So, if your cousin and niece both want the heirloom ring your grandmother left to you and neither backs down, your estate will continue to pay court fees until the matter is resolved. And that's just for one ring.

Let me give you a concrete example from California, where I practice, to show you just how expensive probate can get. The average home value in California is now around $829,000.[8] Yet until very recently, the threshold for real estate going through probate was about $185,000—meaning virtually every homeowner in the state without an estate plan was guaranteed to put their family through the expensive, public probate process.[9] It's recently been changed to allow homes valued at $750,000 or less to go through a "simplified" probate procedure, but that is still less than the average home value. And "simplified" doesn't mean free or fast.

Want to know what this costs families? In California, probate costs can be around 5% to 7% of the market value of assets. Assuming an average home value of $829,000, we're looking at probate costs ranging from $41,000 to $58,000—and that's just

---

8 "California Housing Market," Redfin, 2025, https://www.redfin.com/state/California/housing-market.

9 Shashank Shekhar, "California Median Home Price by County," InstaMortgage, September 4, 2024, https://instamortgage.com/california-median-home-price-by-county-updated-august-2025/.

for your house. If you have other assets, the probate fees will be even higher. That's a year of college tuition, a new car, or a down payment on another house. Just gone.

When people see numbers like these, it suddenly hits them that their own parents probably haven't planned for the future, either. That's when I get one of the most awkward questions: "how do I convince my parents to do an estate plan?" They're not even calling about their own plan; they're calling about their parents' plan. They've realized how much probate will cost, and these adult children are panicking about what it means for their family.

My response is always the same: "have you done your plan yet?" The answer is pretty much always no.

Here's my advice: create your own plan first. That way, when you approach them, you're not coming across as the child asking about the money you'll inherit when they die. You're approaching them as a responsible adult who's done the right thing, asking if they've also done the responsible adult thing.

Imagine being able to say: "Mom, Dad, I just went through the estate planning process. It wasn't as bad as I thought it would be. What was your experience like? Oh, you haven't done it yet? Wow." That conversation hits differently than "Hey, have you guys thought about what happens when you die?" The first approach demonstrates leadership and care, while the second sounds like you're planning their funeral.

Even worse, since probate is public, anyone can pull court records to see what you owned, what debts you left behind, and who's fighting over what. It's practically a treasure map for unscrupulous predators looking to take advantage of the vulnerable. In Palm Beach, Florida, an individual calling himself Jose Suarez contacted residents, identified himself as a lawyer, told them that they were entitled to probate money, and said he would get it for them for a simple $250 fee.[10] And just as with most "recovery" scams (where scammers promise to retrieve lost money for a fee), once Suarez was paid, he ghosted his victims. And in Smith County, Texas, scammers used probate records to identify individuals named in probate cases and sent emails asking for similar "fees."[11]

Some businesses profit from the public availability of probate filings. Since there's limited court oversight in Las Vegas, just about anyone, even complete strangers to the recently deceased person's family, can run a probate case.[12] In 2011, Nevada created an "independent administration" option that was meant to help families speed through the probate process and save them, as well as the court, time and money. However, this law created a loophole that allowed people with no connection to the deceased or their families to claim ownership of the home. These "probate administrators" typically worked with the same investors, real estate agents, and lawyers to sell homes that would later be flipped and sold for a profit, which usually didn't make its way back to the pockets of the estate's heirs.

---

10 "Recovering Money from Probate Cases," Clerk of the Circuit Court & Comptroller, Palm Beach County, https://www.mypalmbeachclerk.com/about-us/news/fraud-alerts/recovering-money-from-probate-cases.

11 "Sheriff Warns of Civil Probate Scam in Smith County," *Tyler Morning Telegraph*, June 24, 2025, https://tylerpaper.com/2025/06/24/sheriff-warns-of-civil-probate-scam-in-smith-county/?utm_source=chatgpt.com.

12 Eli Segall and Michael Scott Davidson, "Lost Legacy," *Las Vegas Review-Journal*, February 9, 2024, https://www.reviewjournal.com/investigations/selling-dead-peoples-homes-lucrative-for-some-but-what-about-the-heirs-2986851/.

It's not hard to find the probate filings for someone you don't know. Simply read the obituaries, pick a random person, note where they lived, ask the county clerk in that area which court handled the probate, and use that information to look up the records either online or at the courthouse. (Why do I suddenly feel like I've just written the equivalent of "here's how to build a bomb"?)

I say that estate planning is an act of love for a reason. It will help your loved ones navigate the worst time of their lives and may keep their private information out of the hands of those who would eagerly take advantage of their grief.

Of course, if you don't like your family all that much, you could be like Mr. Heckles in *Friends* and leave them a whole disaster area to deal with when you're gone. Remember Mr. Heckles? He lived just below Monica and Rachel, and he always complained about their noise to the extent that he referred to them in his will as "the noisy girls in the apartment above mine." He left everything he had to them, and at first, the girls were touched and thought that maybe he really did like them after all. But when they walked into his place, which was a cluttered mess of clothes, newspapers, and random junk, Monica exclaimed, "Would you look at this dump? He hated us. This is his final revenge!"[13]

But since you've read this far, I'm going to assume that you *do* love your family, so let's discuss what I mean by "holistic estate plan," and why getting one is a good choice for people like us.

---

13 *Friends*, season 2, episode 3, "The One Where Heckles Dies," written by David Crane, Marta Kauffman, and Michael Curtis, directed by Kevin Bright, aired October 5, 1995, on NBC.

How Is a Holistic Estate Plan Different?

Simply put, "holistic" means looking at the full picture and not just at the isolated parts.

It's like when you build your character in *Mass Effect*. As with many BioWare games, your choices as you play *Mass Effect* influence the relationships you have with the NPCs (non-playable characters) you interact with throughout the playthrough. During the game, you'll have options to make Paragon ("good guy") or Renegade ("bad guy") choices, which may be met with praise or hostility by your squadmates (the team of NPCs who accompany you throughout the game's storyline). Make too many Renegade (or Paragon) choices, and you risk alienating or even permanently losing squadmates, which can be a huge detriment when you reach certain boss battles.

Maxing out your Renegade points might give you that unique dialogue option for an unforgettable cutscene, but it can also affect how your squadmates interact with you. The overall negative impact on your squadmates' loyalty can determine whether they survive the final mission. Without building strong and balanced relationships with your squad, understanding the political landscape, and making choices that align with the outcome you *actually* want, the whole mission falls apart.

Traditional estate planning is akin to a fragmented skill tree. You'll get a trust, a will, and maybe some powers of attorney (the legal equivalent of *Mass Effect's* biotic powers, tech upgrades, and a souped-up shotgun). But there's no *cohesive strategy*. No one's helping you think through how it all fits

together or what happens when life throws you a curveball...
or a Reaper invasion.

Holistic estate planning is like building your best Paragon or
Renegade run—one where your team knows what's coming,
your assets are aligned with your goals, and your legacy is clear.
It's not just about the documents. It's about *planning for real life*,
and ensuring your loved ones aren't scrambling through your
inventory trying to guess which button to push next.

I don't mean to preemptively gatekeep, but this *is* the "before it
was cool" moment of your adulting arc.

Most people don't realize estate planning can be this
thoughtful, this strategic, or even this human. They think it's
just paperwork and probate. But once you see the full picture,
you can't unsee it. When your friends are still downloading
fill-in-the-blank forms or crossing their fingers with a free will
(or, as is too often the case, relying on crowdfunding to help
their families pay the bills), you'll already be light-years ahead
with a plan that actually works in real life.

You know what's funny? Many traditional estate planning
attorneys get kind of judgy about how I do things. They
don't get why I'm spending hours getting to know my clients,
walking them through their options, and making sure their
plan actually works when their family needs it. They wonder
why I bother explaining the "why" behind every decision, or
why I care about what legacy means beyond money. To them,
that's all a waste of valuable attorney time. After all, they think
that a lawyer's job is to sell the documents, collect the flat fee,
and move on. That's what many estate planning attorneys were

trained to do. Because in their world, estate planning is just a stack of documents. Quick. Transactional. Impersonal.

Now, let's be real: the attorney-client relationship *is* transactional. It's a business, and we all have bills to pay. But when estate planning is *only* transactional, something gets lost. You're not using the attorney as a counselor-at-law. You're delegating the task of creating legal documents to them.

You give up your voice.

Think about it. If you're in a trial, you rely on your attorney to develop the best strategy because you want one outcome: to WIN. Your job is mainly to tell your side of the story and let the attorney handle the strategy. But estate planning is much more personal. There's no single "right" answer, only what's right for you and your family. That's why, as a lawyer, I need to understand your values, your relationships, your fears, your dreams. You're not just hiring me to execute a strategy; we're collaborating to create a plan that reflects who you are and what matters most to you.

When you delegate document creation, you're treating one of the most important decisions of your life like ordering takeout. You're missing out on the opportunity to think deeply about your legacy, have conversations with your family, and ensure your plan actually works when it matters most.

Traditional estate planning lawyers aren't inherently bad or malicious; the system that's been taught for decades is fundamentally flawed. Law school trains us to spot patterns and prescribe solutions based on facts, but there are no clean "fact patterns" when it comes to real people and their real lives.

And that's *exactly* the problem.

At networking events, I often hear, "I've never heard an attorney talk about estate planning the way you do." That's because I don't fit the mold.

This approach is disruptive—intentionally so.

It challenges the outdated idea that estate planning is merely a set of documents. The traditional way of doing estate planning leaves families with stacks of paper and no guidance. My firm puts relationships first. It's personal. It's empowering. And it's designed to actually work when your loved ones need it most.

Holistic estate planning is relational, not transactional, and it begins with an attorney who listens to you and takes your concerns and desires seriously. I previously mentioned that I'm part of a national organization called Personal Family Lawyer®, which is dedicated to helping you create the exact plan that you and your family need through relational lawyering. As a holistic estate planning attorney, I don't just draft documents; I build lasting relationships. If something happens to you, I want your loved ones to feel supported, not burdened with a pile of confusing paperwork.

Here's an overview of my process:

- **Discovery Call:** This is a quick call to discuss your goals, concerns, and what you hope to accomplish. I'll also explain how my process works so you can decide if we're a good fit.
- **Life & Legacy Planning Session:** This is where we design your plan together. I'll help you understand how the law

applies to your specific situation, walk you through your options, and guide you in creating a plan that truly fits your life, values, and legacy.

- **Signing Meeting:** Once your documents are ready, we'll schedule a notary to come to your home (or another convenient location) to ensure all documents are properly signed and officially in place.
- **Legacy Interview:** After your plan is signed, you'll record a special message for your loved ones. It's a way for your voice, your stories, and your values to be passed down along with your assets.
- **Plan Delivery & Maintenance Phase:** You'll receive your completed Life & Legacy Plan portfolio along with personalized guidance on how to align your assets with the plan. This marks the beginning of the maintenance phase—because your plan should evolve as your life does.
- **Three-Year Check-In:** I'll follow up in three years to ensure your plan still reflects your life, your wishes, and your loved ones' needs. If anything has changed, we'll update it together.

This snapshot doesn't do the process justice because it's so much more than a few simple stages. The Life & Legacy Planning Session is at the heart of the process, and it centers on understanding your unique needs as much as possible. I ask questions about the people and things you want to protect, the people you want to name as guardians or trustees, and the story you want to preserve in your estate. Traditional attorneys may neglect to ask if your chosen trustee can handle conflict, but I will. After all, if your sister thinks your child's trust money should be spent in ways that go against your wishes, you don't want a trustee who will give in to her demands just because they're afraid to say no.

I'll guide you through a Legacy Interview, a recorded conversation that captures your voice, your heart, and the wisdom only you can pass on. I will also help you craft a Legacy Letter (sometimes called an ethical will), which is a written message filled with your hopes, lessons, and the love you want those you care about to carry forward for years to come. Through this video and letter, you'll be able to share what you love most about your loved ones, the hopes you carry for their future, and the values you want them to remember.

Holistic estate planning also includes caring for your digital life. Your photos, personal videos, social media profiles, video channels (YouTube, Twitch, etc.), gaming libraries and in-game digital assets, crypto wallets, domain names, online businesses, and more are all part of your story—part of you that's worth preserving. They're the type of things a traditional attorney won't think to ask about, and the type of thing many of us may feel uncomfortable mentioning for fear of being seen as "weird."

The Story You're Afraid to Tell Deserves a Plan Too

Even those of us who feel completely at ease in our nerdy identities don't like to feel judged. It's this fear of being judged that keeps people from telling traditional attorneys what they truly want when it comes to their final wishes. Add that fear to the fact that most attorneys *aren't* going to ask the right questions, and the result is silence. Stories aren't preserved or, at least, told the way they should be told.

I love holistic estate planning because of the human connections I make. I get to ask questions about someone's life story and learn who they are. And when we can bond over a shared fandom? Even better.

Recently, I worked with a fellow Star Wars fan to design his estate plan. The fact that our Life & Legacy Planning Session was a conversation about who he was and what he cared about, rather than just a review of what he owns and who he wants to leave it to, created a safe space where he felt comfortable expressing himself and articulating what he truly wants. He told me that if he ever has to be taken off life support, he wants someone to say, "May the Force be with you" as he passes, and that he wants to have his ashes scattered among the redwoods where *Return of the Jedi* was filmed. I think it's so beautiful that he felt that he could be his authentic self with me.

That's the same level of comfort I want for you too. I'm not going to judge you for who you are, who and what you love, or how you want to be remembered. No one—especially the lawyer you turn to for estate planning—should do that. Too many of us have spent so much of our lives hiding our stories to fit in with everyone else. We definitely shouldn't feel like we have to do that in the hereafter as well.

Knowing what estate planning can do—how it can honor your values, protect your people, and reflect your real life—makes it all the more frustrating that so many people never take the first step. Often, it's not because they don't care; it's because they've been told the wrong story. But before they can even get started, they have to move past the myths holding them back. Those myths are what we will discuss next.

Chapter 2

From Myth to Reality— Estate Planning Isn't Just for the Rich and Famous

Sometimes, rich people think more about money
than they do about people.

–Rose Nylund, *The Golden Girls*

In the late 1980s and early 1990s, the TV show *Lifestyles of the Rich and Famous* welcomed Americans into the opulent homes of the superrich. I remember Robin Leach's booming, nasal voice telling us the stories of people who lived on "champagne wishes and caviar dreams" as the camera panned across private jets, leather couches with gilded wood accents, and dining room tables almost overflowing with fine china and delicate crystal glassware. These people lived the type of lives the rest of us would only experience vicariously. But even as kids watching that show, we knew something was different about these people. They had *systems*. Teams of people managing their lives, their money, and their legacies. They had plans for their plans. Watching the show, you just knew their kids, grandkids, and even their great-grandkids would be set for the rest of their lives.

But here's the thing: just because someone is rich doesn't mean they're a financial genius. Countless rich and famous people have made poor decisions regarding their estates. Take, for example, former Zappos CEO Tony Hsieh. A Harvard-educated computer scientist, Hsieh sadly succumbed to injuries he received in a house fire in 2020. For five years after his death, his family believed he hadn't left a will specifying how to handle his $500 million estate. Then, in a perfect made-for-TV moment, a mystery will surfaced in the spring of 2025.

This will, dated five years before his passing, has thrown the processing of his estate into even further turmoil. While there haven't been any reports of fistfights between the litigants involved, I wouldn't be surprised to see the scriptwriters who adapt his story for Netflix add in a few.

Sadly, too many people choose not to create an estate plan, leaving their loved ones to face the kind of chaos Hsieh's family is currently experiencing. And while we may never know why Hsieh didn't leave a clearly defined estate plan, there are plenty of reasons why the average person might avoid doing so. In this chapter, I'm going to break down the common myths and misconceptions that discourage people from creating an estate plan and show you why it's so crucial to get started on yours now.

Myth #1: "I'm Too Young to Need an Estate Plan"
Truth: You Don't Need to Be a Golden Girl

One main reason people don't create estate plans is that they think they're too young. Wills and estate plans are for our parents and grandparents, right? They're for people like the ladies in *The Golden Girls* who were retired and accepted that they weren't getting any younger. (Except for Blanche Devereaux—she would never admit to getting older.) However, estate planning isn't about your age; it's about the outcome you want in a worst-case scenario.

I get it—you don't *feel* old. You're out there doing life, juggling responsibilities, maybe raising kids or a dog or just yourself, and that's plenty. Whether you're partnered, single, building wealth, paying off student loans, or finally figuring out what you want to be when you grow up, this still applies to you.

Estate planning isn't only about your age or relationship status, nor is it always about preparing for what will happen after you die. It's also about being in control of what happens, even when you can't speak for yourself. Consider what happened to Tony Hsieh. Let's say that he didn't succumb to his injuries but instead was incapacitated in the hospital for weeks or months after that fire. Since he didn't have an estate plan, no one would have been able to make medical decisions on his behalf. Did he have a do-not-resuscitate (DNR) order? Did he want to donate his organs? Was there someone who had access to his financial information to simply ensure that his bills were paid on time? Who knows?

If you're ever in a similar situation, who will step in if you can't speak for yourself? Who will have access to your accounts or belongings? You don't need a spouse, kids, or a lot of money in the bank to make planning for these kinds of situations worthwhile. If you have *people* you care about, *wishes* you want honored, or *preferences* for how your story plays out—that's all it takes to justify creating an estate plan.

And if you think you're too young for an estate plan, think again. Michelle Trachtenberg, who played Buffy's younger sister in the cult classic *Buffy the Vampire Slayer*, was only 39 when she tragically and suddenly passed away due to complications from diabetes. For millennials especially, Michelle wasn't just an actress. She was *Harriet the Spy*, the determined 11-year-old detective in our childhood living rooms. She was Dawn Summers in *Buffy the Vampire Slayer*, Georgina Sparks in *Gossip Girl*, and the relatable younger sister in *EuroTrip*. Here was someone who grew up in front of us, someone who felt like part of our extended friend group through the screen. If this tragedy could happen to her, a young, successful woman with every reason to believe she had decades ahead of her, it can happen to any of us. Having lost her at such a young age, we are reminded of something easily forgotten in our busy lives: there's no "right age" to start thinking about protecting ourselves and the people we love.

Many of us put off estate planning, imagining it as something for later: after the kids are grown, after the mortgage is paid, or after retirement. We picture it as the epilogue to a long and fulfilling life rather than an essential thread woven throughout our story.

But life doesn't always follow imagined timelines.

Recent health statistics for Gen Xers and millennials tell a concerning story, with heart attacks increasing by 2% annually among Americans under 40[14] and some types of cancer rates running two to three times higher than for previous generations.[15]

Those aren't just numbers. They're a wake-up call that asks: what would happen to the people who depend on your presence, love, and support if tomorrow turns out drastically different from what you expected?

As much as we hate to admit it, every story has an end. Honestly, I hate endings. There are video games and TV series I've never finished because I just don't want them to end. It's ironic that I wound up in this field and love it as much as I do considering how I feel about endings. But I've come to accept that as much as I hate endings and as much as I want everybody's story to be a never-ending story, that's just not possible.

It's important to remember that age and death aren't the only reasons you need to create an estate plan. Unlike a will, which *only* kicks in when you die, an estate plan can step in to take care of things when you're alive and unable to make legal decisions (and in some cases, unable to physically take care of yourself). In the legal world, we refer to this state as "incapacity." Outside of the legal world, most people refer to it as being incapacitated.

When I mention "incapacitated," what's the first thing that comes to mind? If you're like most people, you probably think

---

14 "COVID-19 Surges Linked to Spike in Heart Attacks," *Cedars Sinai* (blog), October 24, 2022, https://www.cedars-sinai.org/newsroom/covid-19-surges-linked-to-spike-in-heart-attacks/.

15 "What Gen-Xers and Millennials Should Know About Cancer Risk," American Cancer Society, August 20, 2024, https://www.cancer.org/cancer/latest-news/what-gen-xers-and-millennials-should-know-about-cancer-risk.html.

of a coma—that dramatic medical emergency we've seen in countless movies and TV shows. Yes, a coma is incapacitating, but it's also something that doesn't happen often. At any given moment, around 31 in 100,000 people in the US are in a coma (meaning approximately 102,000 people in the US are in a coma currently). That's only 0.03% of the population. Statistically speaking, you're unlikely to ever be in a coma. So why should you worry about being incapacitated?

What if I told you that a coma is only one way someone can be incapacitated? In legal terms, a person doesn't have to be unconscious to be considered incapacitated. Simply put, "incapacitated" refers to someone who is physically or mentally incapable of managing their own affairs.

Commonplace events, such as car or workplace accidents, incapacitate hundreds of thousands of Americans each year. Likewise, medical conditions such as stroke, severe head trauma, dementia, and Alzheimer's, and mental health disorders such as depression, schizophrenia, and psychosis can all cause incapacity. We like to think that we'll never experience any of these situations, but unless you've developed an X factor and have received your invitation letter to join the X-Men and attend Charles Xavier's School for Gifted Youngsters, the statistical chances of you being incapacitated are much higher than you think.

If you became incapacitated, who would be legally allowed to make medical decisions on your behalf? If you were in the hospital, who would the staff listen to when deciding the best course of action? Your spouse or partner? Your parents? Your BFF, Jill?

If you're estranged from your spouse and don't get along with your parents, you'd probably want the hospital staff to listen to Jill. But guess what? They won't. Your spouse will be their first choice, and if they're not available, your parents will be their second choice. Unless Jill has your medical power of attorney, she won't have any legal standing to make medical decisions for you, even if she's the person you'd choose.

Picture this nightmare scenario: you're unconscious, and your estranged spouse, the one who cheated on you, is deciding whether you get the experimental treatment or the conservative approach. Or maybe your parents, who still think your girlfriend is "just a phase," are making decisions about your care while the person who actually knows your wishes is sitting helplessly in the waiting room.

Who will be the one to decide? A judge. And you definitely don't want a random judge deciding who gets to make life-altering decisions for you.

Your estate plan is like insurance for your life story. You don't have to be *old* to protect your legacy or decide who's going to be your go-to when the going gets tough. You just have to be *adulting*. And if you're already managing a mortgage, curating the ultimate Funko collection, figuring out how to keep a tiny human alive, or having any meaningful relationships at all, guess what? You're adulting hard enough to need a plan.

So, no, estate planning isn't just for the ultra-wealthy or the *Golden Girls*. It's for you—right now, exactly as you are.

Myth #2: "I Don't Have Enough Stuff to Need a Plan"

Truth: If You Own Anything, You Have an Estate

Let's face it. Without a winning lottery ticket or being miraculously included in a multimillionaire's hidden will, most of us are unlikely to become rich and famous. And that's okay. However, what's not okay is that many people believe they don't have an estate simply because they don't live in a mansion, own a yacht, or drive a Bugatti. Remember, it's not about how much you have; it's about where what you have goes when you're gone.

Many people think, "I don't have an estate, so there's nothing to plan." But if you have stuff—any stuff—you have an estate. It's that simple.

I'm not just referring to collections of mint condition Star Wars figures or first edition comic books here. Sure, you want to leave clear instructions about who will receive the collections you've spent hundreds of dollars on and what they should do if they decide to sell them. But even if you don't have a valuable collection, you have *stuff*. If you own *anything*—your home, a bank account, the vintage vinyl collection you cherish, a cat with an attitude, and even digital photos and social media accounts—you already have enough to warrant calling your possessions an estate.

Take a moment and look around you. I know, I know. You're thinking, "But, my stuff isn't worth anything." But it's not about the dollar value. It's about the story. That signed poster you got at your first Comic-Con? Those program guides from all those early 2000s conventions? The DVD box sets you refuse to get rid of? That gaming setup you've carefully curated? The thousands of photos on your phone from conventions, game nights, and that epic cosplay photoshoot? The screenshots of funny tweets, important text conversations, and that one meme that perfectly sums up your entire personality? Someone has to decide what happens to all of it.

What do you see? In my living room, I see a flat-screen TV, an Xbox, my DVD box sets of *Angel*, *Buffy*, *Battlestar Galactica* (and more), my husband's Macross collectibles, a Bose sound system, the laptop I'm writing on, a room full of furniture, and a bunch of knickknacks. That's an abbreviated list of the things in just one room in my house. When I'm gone, someone will have to deal with all of that. Who's going to get the TV, consoles, computers, and so on? Who's going to sell, donate, or discard the rest?

What happens after we're gone *matters*.

It matters to the people we love, to the world we've helped shape, and to the story we leave behind. While some of us may not have much money, a priceless collection, a home, or a car, we all have possessions we care about, and people we want to receive those possessions when we pass on. A solid estate plan will not only ensure that the things you love go to the right people, but it will also help them understand what to do with the rest of your stuff too. It's the after-credits scene that allows you to step into the story one more time and make the transition to the next chapter of their lives as easy as possible for your loved ones.

Myth #3: "I Just Want Something Simple"

Truth: A Simple Will Doesn't Keep Your Family Out of Court

Everyone I've ever talked to has told me that they "just need something simple" for their estate plan. But what they *really* mean is that they want things to be as simple as possible for their loved ones if something were ever to happen to them. However, a simple will usually doesn't lead to a simple outcome. And it doesn't avoid probate—it almost guarantees it.

When you consider the problems associated with letting your estate go to probate (taxes, legal fees, court costs, along with the emotional strain of sorting through your possessions, finances, and everything else you leave after you're gone), you'll realize that an estate plan is the key to making things as simple as possible for the people you leave behind.

Estate planning is about making decisions now so your loved ones don't have to clean up a legal mess later. And honestly? Court costs from not planning can far exceed what a good plan would have cost. But here's a question you might not have thought about yet: would probate-related costs and court costs create a burden for your loved ones?

If you're like me (and if you're reading this book, you probably are), you are likely part of what's been called the "sandwich generation." We're millennials and Gen Xers who are "frequently caught between raising children and caring for aging parents." After the loss of a family member, we typically "face the steepest costs financially, professionally, and emotionally."[16]

Empathy, an organization dedicated to supporting people burdened by the loss of loved ones, researched the various ways grief can impact our lives. In 2025, they released the "The Grief Tax" report, which breaks down the cost of dying in America. They discovered that 54% of the people they surveyed "used their own money to cover post-loss costs," and that many of them used credit cards or loans to do so, which increased their "risk of prolonged and severe financial hardship."

Even if you have money in your account that could cover your final expenses, without an estate plan, your loved ones won't be able to access it for months or even years. The rules are rigid, the paperwork is endless, and the people making the decisions? They're total strangers. Your assets will be placed into probate and managed according to the state's default plan. It's called intestacy law, and it decides who gets what, when, and how—all with zero input from you. It doesn't care about your relationships, your values, or that one cousin you've mentally unfollowed in real life.

If you're imagining that this will be handled quickly and efficiently, think again. Remember the DMV scene from *Zootopia* where Flash the sloth takes an eternity to type a single word and laugh at a joke? That's the kind of speed we're talking about. Bureaucratic. Slow. Painfully impersonal. Meanwhile, your loved ones are stuck waiting, paying court fees, and

---

16 "The Grief Tax," Empathy, 2025, https://www.empathy.com/thegrieftax.

navigating a bureaucratic maze at the exact moment they're actively grieving.

Many of those who haven't experienced the loss of a loved one (or know someone who has) are unaware of the financial burdens that can arise when there's no estate plan. And unfortunately, those who are aware often turn to free or inexpensive online will sites because they just want to create a quick, simple document that will take care of their family and won't break the bank.

They do an internet search for "free will plans" and find sites that claim they can "Make a Will for Free in Less Than 20 Minutes." Some even state that they can help you "Create a Trust-Based Plan" for the low, low price of $349! But the problem with these "one-size-fits-all" plans is that they don't fit all, and they certainly won't fit you. And they won't grow with you or check in on you every few years to ensure that the plan you started with is the one you want to keep using. Ask yourself: what was your life like five years ago? Do you have the same priorities as you did then? The same assets, family, friends, pets, bills, and so on? If you created a low-cost will back then, would it cover everything it needs to cover today?

While the free will site you just clicked on claims it can help your family avoid probate, the truth is that it probably won't. If the plan you created with them is outdated, if it doesn't cover contingencies, if it doesn't point out that things like your life insurance aren't automatically included in the will, and so on, guess what? It's going to probate, and your family might end up having to fight over what hasn't already been eaten by court costs and lawyer fees.

Myth #4: "My Family Will Know What to Do"

Truth: If You Don't Tell Them Now, They'll Be Guessing Later

And it's not just about the money or things you'll leave behind. If you're incapacitated, decisions about your care will be complicated.

You might be tempted to say, "My family knows what to do. It'll be fine." But when was the last time you sat down with your family and really discussed your wishes? It's a difficult conversation to have. I mean, who sits at the breakfast table and says, "Hey, sweetie? If I'm ever so brain damaged that I don't know who I am, please don't keep me on a feeding tube, OK?" Being incapacitated involves more than deciding whether or not to "pull the plug." If you assume your family will know your wishes, you're just forcing them to guess, which adds a huge emotional burden during what is already the worst time of their lives. What's even worse is the fact that your family members may not see eye to eye when it comes to deciding what's best for you and your children.

In 1990, Terri Schiavo was hospitalized after a severe heart attack, and the resulting complications from a significant loss of oxygen to her brain put her in a persistent vegetative state.[17] Her husband argued that she told him that she didn't "want to be kept alive on a machine," and after three years, he decided to remove her from life support. Terri's parents, on the other hand, argued that her doctors were wrong and sued for control

---

17 Charles Weijer, "A Death in the Family: Reflections on the Terri Schiavo Case," *Canadian Medical Association Journal* 172, no. 9 (April 2005), https://doi.org/10.1503/cmaj.050348.

over her medical decisions. Their ensuing legal battle triggered a nationwide debate about a person's right to life and family rights regarding maintaining an individual's life support.

Like Schiavo's parents, some of your family members may disagree with your medical team's diagnosis and want to continue treatment even if that contradicts your wishes. On the other hand, they may want to end treatment even if *that* decision contradicts your wishes. Or they may simply want to change the type of treatment you're receiving (think of assisted living vs. in-home care, for example).

Don't forget what I said earlier: you don't need to be in a coma or a persistent vegetative state to be incapacitated. Incapacity comes in many forms, and you want to make sure that the person in charge of your care (which can include the care of your children, home, pets, and finances) is the person *you* choose, not the person a court believes is the best choice.

Don't believe me? Just ask Britney Spears. Her story illustrates that in some cases, the court's decision to side with a person's next of kin isn't always the right choice. In February 2008, after her famous head-shaving incident and her assault of a paparazzi's car with an umbrella, a California court placed her under a "temporary" conservatorship, which was controlled by her father. Her ordeal didn't end until November 2021.[18] For nearly 14 years, she had no control over her finances, was forced to take lithium, and was even refused the right to remove her IUD (intrauterine device) because her conservators "did

---

18 Loren Barr, "Britney Spears Conservatorship Case Explained," Barr & Douds Attorneys, June 27, 2025, https://www.barrattorneys.com/blog/britney-spearss-conservatorship-case-explained/.

not want her to get pregnant." It's no wonder she described the experience as a "nightmare."

This is what happens when you don't choose who speaks for you. Britney had millions of dollars and a team of lawyers, and yet she still couldn't escape a conservatorship that controlled every aspect of her life for over a decade. What do you think would happen to you or me?

Britney Spears' father definitely wasn't the person she wanted to take control of her health and finances. I doubt she wanted him to make decisions for her kids, either. If Britney's story teaches us anything, it's that your family won't always make the best decisions for you, even if they have the best of intentions.

Myth #5: "My Spouse or Kids Will Automatically Get Everything"

Truth: Legal Ownership Isn't Always as Simple as It Looks

Just like you can't assume your family will know your wishes (or even adhere to them), you can't assume that everything you have will automatically be given to them after your passing.

At first glance, this myth appears to make sense. After all, who else would a court decide to give everything to? But when you look deeper, you'll realize that it's not so simple. Sadly, death never is.

Your circumstances will change over time. You may have more kids, find a new partner, buy a house, or start a business—the list is endless. And if your estate plan doesn't account for these changes, your belongings and finances may not necessarily go to the people you intend.

I receive many calls that sadly come when it's too late to do anything. One came from a young man whose aunt had just died. He provided her end-of-life care and while she was alive, they visited a free will site and designed a will that essentially stated, "I leave everything to my nephew." After she passed, her entire life insurance policy went to her brother, whom she hadn't spoken to in over ten years.

Why? Because a will does not determine who receives life insurance benefits. They didn't know that her assets needed to be legally aligned with her plan to create the outcome she wanted. Like most of us, she thought things would be like you always see in movies, where someone says everything goes to this person, and boom! It does.

But it *doesn't* work that way.

She needed to change her life insurance beneficiary, which isn't something an online estate planning site, credit union, or financial planning app will necessarily tell you. Estate planning is more than just finding a form, filling it out, and signing it. It's a comprehensive approach to ensuring that your assets go where you want them to when you die. And making sure that you are cared for by the person you select in the way that you want if you become incapacitated.

Retirement benefits are also overlooked when people attempt to DIY their estate plans, use free or inexpensive online will planning tools, or even use the services offered by their bank or credit union. Take Jeff Rolison, for example. He had been employed by Procter & Gamble for years when he decided to name his girlfriend as the beneficiary of his retirement plan.[19] When they parted ways after a two-year relationship, he didn't remove her as his beneficiary. As a result, when he passed away 35 years after they broke up, she was still listed on the paperwork. His account, which was worth over $750,000 when he passed away in 2015, is now locked in escrow as his family and ex-girlfriend continue to fight it out in court.

Your assets may not automatically flow to where you'd naturally expect them to, and if you don't have an experienced estate attorney on your side, things like insurance benefits and retirement accounts can slip through the cracks and land in some unexpected places.

It sounds a little weird when I say it out loud, but even houses can slip through the cracks. I knew someone whose mom remarried and bought her dream house with her new husband. Unfortunately, they separated, and because of the way the house was titled, when she passed from COVID, nothing went to her kids. He and his kids, however, are enjoying that nice house.

I'm sure this all feels a little overwhelming. After all, there are so many different elements involved in creating a thorough and useful estate plan that you must be thinking you'll never be able to create one. But that's why I wrote this book. I'm here to guide you through the scenarios that may arise and help you

---

19 Anna Sulkin Stern, "Ex-Girlfriend May Get Windfall Due to Beneficiary Designation Snafu," *WealthManagement.com*, June 26, 2024, https://www.wealthmanagement.com/estate-planning/ex-girlfriend-may-get-windfall-due-to-beneficiary-designation-snafu

discover thoughtful approaches to shield the people and things you love from unnecessary hardship.

So, what's our first stop? It's 4 Privet Drive and the cupboard under the stairs, of course!

Chapter 3

Don't Let Dumbledore Decide—Plan Now to Protect Your Children Later

The consequences of our actions are always so complicated,
so diverse, that predicting the future is a very
difficult business indeed.

—J.K. Rowling, *Harry Potter and the Order of the Phoenix*

As the parents of one of the two boys who could fulfill Sybill Trelawney's prophecy and kill Voldemort for good, Lily and James Potter had to know that their lives would be at risk until the prophecy was fulfilled and either Voldemort or Harry was dead. Like many other characters who stood against the Dark Lord, Lily and James were high on the Death Eaters' hit list. Why, then, weren't they prepared for the worst? They didn't even lay out a concrete plan for what would happen to their son, Harry, if Voldemort or the Death Eaters got to them.

Perhaps they thought that Harry would be placed with his godfather, Sirius Black, if Death Eaters or Voldemort Avada Kedavra'd them. That makes sense, right? But while the godparent is often expected to fill in as guardian, being a godparent doesn't come with the legal authority to care for someone else's child. When you consider that Sirius Black was in no position to care for Harry while he was imprisoned in Azkaban, it's no wonder that the decision of where Harry would go was left to Dumbledore. After all, he was the Chief Warlock of the Wizengamot and the Supreme Mugwump of the International Confederation of Wizards. You can't find someone more "head honcho" than that at a minute's notice. Most of the wizarding world (Minerva McGonagall and Hagrid notwithstanding) believed that Dumbledore's decision to place Harry with Harry's aunt and uncle was logical, strategic, and arguably justifiable.

But was it the *right* decision?

Like our real-world courts, Dumbledore believed in the greater good and did what he thought was best for Harry.

Does a fancy government title, such as Chief Warlock or Judge, *really* give someone you've never met the right to determine the destiny of your child?

Unfortunately, the answer is yes.

Instead of being raised in a loving home by one of his parents' closest friends, Harry was taken away to be raised by Lily's sister, Petunia Dursley, and her husband Vernon Dursley. And while the Dursleys looked like the perfect middle-class family on paper, they had a deep prejudice against magic, which caused them to waver between neglecting and mistreating Harry.

If you don't have legal documents that express your wishes in the event of your death or incapacity, the court will make decisions it deems to be in the best interests of your child. But that "best interest" might be based on formalities and assumptions like biology, income, and marital status—not love, understanding, and the values you hold dear. It will rely on a *random* person's interpretation of the information provided to them by Child Protective Services (CPS), the police, your friends and family, and so on. At least Dumbledore knew Harry's parents. In the real world, it's unlikely that the deceased will be close friends with the CPS agents who take charge of their children.

If Lily and James had an estate plan, I imagine they probably would have named Minerva McGonagall as Harry's temporary guardian. She, not Dumbledore, would have taken him from Hagrid at the beginning of the story. If they had a trusted legal advisor who would have guided them through the process of creating an emergency plan, they would have identified multiple backups to Sirius Black, such as Remus Lupin, the Longbottoms, and the Weasleys to act as Harry's long-term guardians. They also would have included a clause that stated under no circumstances should Harry be taken to the Dursleys.

People familiar with the series know that Dumbledore placed Harry with the Dursleys because Lily's sacrifice meant that there were protections that lived in Harry's blood, and he needed to be near blood relatives for those protections to work. Fans have argued about the amount of time Harry would have to spend each year with the Dursleys for those protections to stay in place. However, in *Harry Potter and the Order of the Phoenix*, Dumbledore tells Harry that "While you can still call home the place where your mother's blood dwells, there you cannot be touched or harmed by Voldemort....You need return there only once a year."[20] In essence, he could have easily lived with anyone on the Potter's list and simply stayed with the Dursleys a few days a year. And, at some point, he must have stopped considering the Dursleys's place "home." Hogwarts was much more of a home to him.

Dumbledore's decision to permanently place Harry with the Dursleys, even though Petunia clearly hated her sister, likely went against Lily and James's wishes. But because the Potters never wrote down their wishes, no one can really say what would have happened differently for Harry.

The same is true for all parents. No matter how many conversations or good intentions people have in mind, none of that is real until it's put in writing. So until things are written in a properly executed guardian nomination, you don't have the certainty that your best friend would take care of your kid if something ever happens to you.

This is why having written, legal documents that clearly spell out your guardianship instructions is vital. When it comes to the people you love, assumptions about who'll step up during your time of need could very well leave you and your loved ones high and dry. But having a will isn't as ironclad as you might think, which is what we're going to talk about next.

Not Everyone Gets a Mandalorian: Why a Will Isn't Enough

Fans of *The Mandalorian* are familiar with "The Way"—the creed that shapes the choices of the protagonist, Din Djarin,

---

20 J.K. Rowling, *Harry Potter and the Order of the Phoenix* (New York: Scholastic, 2003), 836.

throughout the series. A principal part of his culture is the care of foundlings. They are to be cared for until their parents are found or until they reach adulthood. In fact, the members of his tribe routinely donate funds to cover the costs of raising these children. When he rescues Grogu, AKA Baby Yoda, Din Djarin steps into the role of guardian and eventually adopts the child as his own.

If only reality worked the same way. Parents wouldn't need to worry about what would happen if they died or became incapacitated. Their children would be cared for by a community dedicated to their well-being. However, even if you live in such a community, without an estate plan, no one will have the legal authority to care for your children until the courts appoint a guardian, even if those caring individuals are ready to step up.

Don't get me wrong. A will is an important document for protecting minor children. It enables you to name a guardian (or guardians) for your children upon your death. But that's pretty much the extent of what it can do. And most importantly, it *only* kicks in after you die.

That's why a will alone can't ensure that your children stay with someone you want them to if you're hospitalized. A will won't identify who can and can't make medical decisions on behalf of your children or provide access to your finances so the person with whom they're placed can cover their expenses. On the other hand, a *comprehensive* estate plan allows you to name a short-term guardian who can be an emergency responder and has the legal authority to care for your children in the event of an emergency.

In most cases, when a parent or guardian is incapacitated and unable to care for their children (and the other parent is also unable to provide care), the first thing that will happen is that their children will be taken into CPS custody until a family member or a named guardian can be found. In some cases, this can happen pretty quickly. However, if your closest family member lives several states away or you haven't named a guardian, your child will be placed in a foster home until one is located.

This isn't a fun process. Picture this: your child gets picked up from school by strangers and is taken to another stranger's home without their Baby Yoda plush, their favorite video game, or even time to process what's happening. On the worst day of their lives, they're surrounded by people who don't know that your child is scared of the dark or that they'll only eat a sandwich if it's cut diagonally.

In some cases, the picture I just painted is reality. CPS will pick the child up directly from school and take them directly to a foster home. Sure, they will be able to go home and pack a few things at some point, but in that moment of crisis and confusion, they'll be taken into custody by strangers, brought to another stranger's home (if a home is available), and cut off from the things that bring them comfort during difficult times.

If you haven't named a guardian, the next thing that will happen is that the court will try to locate a family member to place the child with. This is often referred to as "kinship care," and usually it's preferable to placing children in the foster care system. While some courts will place children with close family friends, they prefer to choose family members even if they live hours away or haven't previously been significantly involved in the children's lives.

Now pause and reflect on the reality of your situation. If you were unable to take care of your children due to death or incapacity, who would likely come forward to care for them? Who is the closest relative that the court would most likely choose? Are they the person *you'd* choose?

Here's the uncomfortable truth: the person who comes to mind first might not be the right choice. And that's okay. This isn't about hurt feelings. It's about giving your children the best possible outcome in a worst-case scenario.

Typically, I give parents a scenario like this: "You've both become incapacitated in a car accident. What will happen to your children right now?" Often, when I ask these questions, parents tell me who they'd want as guardians instead of acknowledging the uncomfortable reality of what would *actually* happen. One might say something like, "Oh, my brother will take them." I'll say, "That's great!" And then I'll ask the important questions: How will that happen? Who will know to contact him? Where does he live? Is he in the neighborhood, or does he live out of state? What will happen if he's not available? Does he have the legal authority to take them and make medical decisions on their behalf? Will your brother have access to funds to support your children and himself during this time?

Most of the time, parents don't have answers because they haven't progressed beyond the initial stage of identifying a guardian. And in some cases, one parent will name their brother as their chosen guardian while the other will say, "Wait, I thought my mother would take the kids."

This is a difficult conversation to have, but these questions are absolutely important because they're about your kids, and you need to ensure that the people who end up taking care of your children are the ones *you'd* choose.

In essence, you want to hope for the best but plan for the worst, because the worst is *always* a possibility until you ensure it isn't.

For example, I have a client who lives over ten hours away from her nephews. She adores them, but she wouldn't be the best choice for a guardian since she isn't closely involved in their lives. If her brother and sister-in-law don't have an estate plan that names guardians, the courts would consider her a viable option for guardianship. Further complicating the situation is the fact that one of her nephews has autism spectrum disorder, and she has no experience dealing with that condition. Because she loves her nephews, she'd take them, but it would be an emotionally and financially overwhelming situation that would add further stress and trauma to an already difficult situation.

A basic will, especially a DIY will designed on a low-cost will website, won't help you navigate the complex issues your family (and every family) might face. So, how do you choose guardians for your children? What types of things should you consider? Let's explore what really matters when naming a guardian.

This Is (Not) The Way...to Choose a Guardian

In *The Mandalorian*, choosing a guardian for Grogu was pretty easy. Din Djarin found and rescued him, so he became Grogu's guardian. There was no need to consider things such as Grogu's overall health and emotional needs, Din Djarin's readiness or ability to care for a child, or even whether Din Djarin's values aligned with those of Grogu's parents.

In general, Star Wars tends to make choosing a guardian seem like a simple task. Someone simply needs to say that the kids should be placed with a specific family, and boom, it's done. Take Luke and Leia, for example. Obi-Wan (the last known remaining Jedi) and Bail Organa (a member of Alderaan's royal family and a Republic Senator) decide Luke and Leia's fates without considering what Padmé (or even Anakin—before he joined the dark side) would have wanted.

What's especially curious is that Padmé's parents, Jobal and Ruwee, and even her sister Sola, are still around, yet they're never really considered for guardianship. Much like Dumbledore, Obi-Wan and Bail Organa step in and make big decisions about the children's futures, seemingly without exploring all the options. Fair enough, fans of both sagas might argue that Harry, Luke, and Leia's safety had to come first, but the way those choices were made so quickly and with so little discussion should give us pause.

Of course, it's highly unlikely that you'll need to hide your children from a Sith Lord or He-Who-Must-Not-Be-Named, so you don't need to worry about making an abrupt decision about how to best hide your children from danger. (To be honest, it's probably not a good idea to make abrupt decisions about your child's safety if you can avoid it.)

A key thing to remember is that you need to name more than one guardian. Most plans I review make the common mistake of identifying one option for guardianship. Even if the Potters had named only Sirius Black as Harry's guardian, let's think about how that would have played out. Being accused of and imprisoned for killing Lily and James quickly eliminated him and would have sent Harry straight to the Dursleys. That's why a good plan will name backup guardians.

The anime series *Naruto* illustrates this point even more clearly. A young Naruto is orphaned when his parents, Minato and Kushina, died as heroes while protecting their village from a devastating attack. Before their deaths, they named Jiraiya (a legendary ninja and Minato's beloved mentor) as their son's godfather. But when the time came, Jiraiya didn't step up to take care of his godson. Maybe he felt unprepared for parenthood, maybe he thought his dangerous lifestyle wasn't suitable for a child, or maybe he simply couldn't handle the emotional weight of raising his dead student's son.

Whatever the reason, Jiraiya's decision left Naruto's fate to the Third Hokage, another grandfatherly figure in a position of power who, just like Dumbledore, unilaterally decided what was best for Naruto, all in the name of the greater good. The result? Naruto grew up lonely, ostracized, and essentially raised by the state with his basic needs barely met (he grew up primarily eating cup noodles!). Because of this, he lacked the love, guidance, and emotional support that his parents would have wanted him to receive.

Even if you've never watched the series, Naruto's situation is one anyone can understand: loving parents made a plan, but when their chosen guardian couldn't follow through, the lack of a backup plan left Naruto to bear the consequences.

This *Is The Way*...to Choose a Guardian

Now, let's talk about how you can avoid these mistakes and make well-thought-out decisions about the future of the people you want to protect the most. A key part of that careful planning is deciding who could step in if you weren't there and ensuring you're not relying on just one person to carry that responsibility.

Think of this step like putting together your backup team. List a few people who could step in as guardians, both for the short-term and long-term, and rank them in the order you'd want them to be considered. Base your choices on what matters most to you—not on avoiding hurt feelings. This is about your child's future, not about keeping the peace at the next family reunion.

Remember: you're not ranking the value of the family members or friends you are considering as people. You're deciding who will be the best choices for your children.

Here's where it gets tricky: the first people who come to mind might not mesh with your values or your child's needs and personality. If you've ever watched *Wife Swap*, you've seen how living with the "wrong fit" can make things...interesting.

Do you remember that show? Each episode followed two families who "swapped" mothers for two weeks. The catch? The families held starkly different beliefs, values, and parenting styles. One episode swapped a pastor's wife with an atheist

(Season 2, Episode 11). Another swapped a vegan with a family whose father hunted for their food (Season 2, Episode 9). Yet another episode where a strict disciplinarian was swapped with a permissive parent who "unschooled" her children (Season 7, Episode 4). These episodes illustrate the stark differences in lifestyle, values, and parenting styles that make every family unique. They also show just how important it is to carefully choose the people who will guide your children through the rest of their lives.

So, let's start by first thinking about your values. What's important to you? Are you like Captain America, who valued patriotism and loyalty? Spider-Man, who valued responsibility and overcoming adversity? Wonder Woman, who valued justice and gender equality? Black Panther, who valued independence and overcoming oppression?

Next, grab a pen and write down five to ten things that you value most. Here are some ideas to get you started:

Community	Hard Work	Playfulness
Creativity	Health	Respect
Discipline	Honesty	Spirituality
Education	Kindness	Teamwork

Let's pretend that you chose spirituality, education, community, discipline, and health as your five values. How well-suited are your chosen guardians when it comes to those values? How do these potential guardians feel about religion and spirituality? Do they practice the same faith as you? They don't have to, but they need to value and respect the faith you do (or don't) choose to believe in. If you're a devout Catholic, for example, would your Presbyterian best friend support your children continuing to practice Catholicism? Or if you're not very religious, would your chosen guardian expect your children to go to services with them and practice rites and rituals of their religion (such as celebrating religious holidays and traditions, wearing certain types of clothing, avoiding specific foods, and so on)?

Let's move on to education, because that's also something important to consider. Are your chosen guardians more like Ms. Frizzle from *The Magic School Bus* or Edna Krabappel from *The Simpsons*? Are they likely to be actively involved in your children's education, help with homework and after-school activities, and encourage your children's intellectual growth? Do they value the same types of education you value? For example, if you'd encourage your child to pursue a trade-based education, you want to ensure that your chosen guardians share the same attitude. Likewise, if you want your child to participate in faith-based education, will your chosen guardians support your wishes? Take another look at the list of potential guardians you created and note those who are the least likely to support your educational values. You don't have to cross them off the list just yet, but they should move down toward the bottom.

Another critical issue to consider is where your children will live. This is where it helps to have different guardianship choices based on different situations. If you're briefly incapacitated (let's say you're recovering from a stroke and need to be in rehabilitative care), they'd stay with your designated short-term guardians who likely live in your area. But if you've crossed your final finish line, they'd live where your chosen long-term guardian lives.

Do you want your children to remain in the same community? Some people who have high school-aged children try to keep them in the same community so they can stay with the peers they've grown up with. Others prefer to have their children live with close family, even if those family members live in a different state or country. There are no wrong answers here. What's important is that you choose guardians by considering where you want your children to live, regardless of how close or far it is from where you are right now.

Next, it's time to examine how the guardian you choose will interact with your child when they misbehave. What do you feel about discipline? Do you practice authoritative parenting or lean more toward gentle parenting, like Molly Weasley? Her parenting style is based on empathy, understanding, and clear communication. Rather than focusing on punishment and control, gentle parenting involves setting boundaries, managing emotions, and developing problem-solving skills.

Do you prefer a permissive parenting style, like Regina George's mom in *Mean Girls*, which encourages independence by allowing children to define their own rules about things such as bedtime, homework, and screentime? Perhaps you prefer a stricter approach to parenting and expect your children to follow specific rules and face consequences when they break those rules, like Red Forman in *That '70s Show*.[21]

---

21 Terrence Sanvictores and Magda D. Mendez, "Types of Parenting Styles and Effects on Children," National Library of Medicine, September 18, 2022, https://www.ncbi. nlm.nih.gov/books/NBK568743/.

Take another look at your list. If the guardians you've identified have children, does their parenting style match yours? You may adore your best friend and still not agree with how she parents her children, and that's totally fine. But are you fine with her parenting style shaping your children's lives? And if the guardians you've chosen don't have children, what are their attitudes about parenting? How do they interact with your children?

Last, we come to what could be the most critical issue to consider: your children's health. Their guardians will have to make countless health decisions throughout your children's lives. It should go without saying that they need to share your perspectives on matters such as vaccinations and mental health care, and they need to also be willing to follow your wishes regarding the types of treatments you want your children to receive. But it's also important that your chosen guardians are *able* to follow your wishes. Are they physically capable of helping a child who uses a wheelchair over obstacles? Can they take time off work to care for a child undergoing significant medical treatments? Are they willing to take your child to weekly therapy appointments? My client, the one who has a nephew with special needs, is disabled and wouldn't be prepared to step into a guardian role for her nephew, no matter how much she loves him. This doesn't make her a bad person; it only makes her a bad choice for guardianship.

Take another moment and write down the different health conditions your children currently experience. Then go back to your list of potential guardians. Who is both willing *and* able to attend to your children's medical needs?

More Than a Big Check: Building a Lasting Legacy

When we think about someone being able to take care of our children, the first thing we often think of is money. Money will help your chosen guardians care for your children's needs, but a big mistake many parents make is to focus on money rather than values. The amount of money your chosen guardians have in their bank account is irrelevant. It's *your* job as a parent to make sure that you provide the resources to care for your child through a trust. Plus, if net worth is your only deciding factor when choosing a guardian, you run the risk of placing your children with people who won't love and guide them as you would.

Next, you want to consider the potential conflicts that may arise if your chosen guardian is also in charge of your child's trust. If your child wants to do something with funds from their trust, and their guardian says no, things can get pretty heated and complicated. This is why I recommend that you choose a guardian based on your shared values and then name a *separate* person as the trustee. Why?

This isn't about questioning anyone's integrity; it's about protecting something far more precious than money. Picture this scenario: your chosen guardian is doing an amazing job raising your child until that inevitable teenage moment when your child says something like, "If you really loved me, you'd buy me that car for my 16th birthday!" or "All my friends get to go to Cancun for spring break!" When the same person controls both the parenting decisions and the purse strings, every "no" becomes a potential battle about love, fairness, and what you *really* would have wanted.

By separating these roles, you're giving your chosen guardian a beautiful gift: the ability to be the parental figure your child needs without the added pressure of financial gatekeeping. They can say, "I hear you, and I love you, but the trustee handles those decisions based on what your parents set up." It removes them from being the "bad guy" with money and prevents the most important relationship in your child's life from becoming tangled in financial negotiations. That way, they'll be able to focus on what matters most: nurturing, guiding, and loving your child.

If you want to leave your chosen guardian a separate amount of money to use as they see fit (just as you might with other friends and family), that's perfectly fine. Just make sure that it's clearly separated from what's tied to the support of your child.

But what happens once your child turns 18? Money from your insurance policies, investments, retirement accounts, and savings accounts will fund their trust, and that money will often last beyond the day they legally become adults. You want to ensure you spell out how those funds are to be used to care for your children as they grow up *in addition to* how those funds are to be allocated to them *after* they reach 18.

A holistic estate planning attorney will help you draft specific guidelines for how and when your children will receive the funds from their trusts. An attorney using a traditional estate planning approach or a one-size-fits-all template will provide a generic plan that typically divides up the inheritance among your children into periodic lump sums at designated ages.

Let's say that you have $5 million in insurance, and $4 million of it is designated to go to your only child. Many default distributions use the same cookie-cutter formula: 10% at 21 years old, another 30% at 25, and the remaining balance at 30. I see this often when reviewing an existing estate plan, usually because the attorney never explained to the parents what these percentages would mean in real dollars based on their actual assets.

But this means the child would get $400,000 at 21, $1.2 million at 25, and $2.4 million at 30. What would you have done with $400,000 at 21? Would you have invested it in the stock market, bought a house, opened a retirement account, or paid for school? Sure, some people would do these things, but most of us would probably buy a cool car, upgrade our gaming setup, or maybe splurge on some epic experiences. And then, we could just…coast until the next big payout. It's like living paycheck to paycheck, except instead of waiting for your salary, you're waiting for your inheritance. Why be responsible with $400,000 when you know $1.2 million is coming at 25? And even if you split this between two children, the math isn't much better—$200,000 at 21 is still life-changing money that most people would blow through while waiting for the next installment.

Even worse, if you don't do anything at all, they'll get the whole lump sum when they turn 18. Imagine that. Receiving $4 million at 18. When I was 18, I received a $5,000 settlement from a personal injury lawsuit, and I have no clue what I spent it on. I'm sure I didn't go as overboard as Harry Potter did when he pulled a huge handful of gold coins from his pocket and bought the *entire* snack trolley just to impress his new friend, but considering the fact that I don't recall purchasing anything of value, I probably wasn't much different. If someone had advised me to invest it, I'd have a pretty sweet million-dollar retirement account today. I can't imagine what I'd have done with $4 million.

Getting that kind of money at such a young age can be quite dangerous. For example, when Whitney Houston passed in 2012, she left her $20 million estate to her daughter Bobbi Kristina Brown with the stipulation that she receive the default distribution of 10%, 30%, and 60% at 21, 25, and 30. Bobbi received $2 million when she turned 21. Sadly, she was found unresponsive in her bathtub and didn't live long enough to receive the second installment of her inheritance.[22] Of course, that's a worst-case scenario. But without the right kind of financial education, support, and planning, young beneficiaries are likely to lose everything they receive within a matter of years.

It doesn't matter how much or how little you're leaving your children. The average inheritance is spent in just five short years.[23] These are missed opportunities to invest in their future.

---

22 "Estate Planning: Who Inherited Whitney Houston's Fortune?" ElderLawAnswers, August 5, 2015, https://www.elderlawanswers.com/who-will-inherit-whitney-houstons-fortune-following-bobbi-kristinas-death----and-what-are-the-lessons--15256.

23 Laila Maidan, "The 5 Worst Things You Can do With Your Inheritance According to a Financial Planner," *Business Insider*, May 23, 2024, https://www.businessinsider.com/worst-things-inheritance-financial-planner-2024-5.

Working with a thoughtful estate planning lawyer will enable you to create a trust that clearly designates not only when your children will receive their inheritance, but also *what* they can spend it on. For example, you could indicate that upon reaching age 21, your son can buy a specific type of car, like a truck or an SUV, but not spend it on a supercar like a Ferrari. You can also require that they set aside a certain amount for retirement or a down payment on a house. Doing so will ensure that you're creating opportunities, not pitfalls.

Your estate plan can guide them through the complexities associated with inheriting a large sum of money in a way that a simple will cannot. A holistic estate plan will let you assemble a team (a lawyer, trustee, CPA, and financial advisor) who will ensure that your wishes are met, your children aren't left alone with $4 million burning a hole in their pockets, and your estate plan stays up-to-date with the changes your family will experience over time.

From Rugrats to All Grown Up: Your Estate Plan Should Grow Alongside Them

Kids grow up in the blink of an eye. One day, they're playing with Reptar and planning playground adventures, and the next, they're showing you their newest *Minecraft* build or asking for the car keys. But they aren't the only ones that should develop over time: your estate plan needs to grow alongside them.

When you create a will online, through a financial institution, or with a general practice attorney (a lawyer who handles a broad variety of legal matters), chances are you'll get a one and done document. The website won't call you in a couple of years to see if you need to change your plan, the bank won't remind you that you should ensure the person named as the beneficiary for your retirement account is still the person you want, and the general practice attorney probably won't work with your financial advisor to ensure that your assets are aligned to ensure your plan works as intended.

On the other hand, when an estate planning attorney becomes a trusted advisor to your family, they'll nurture your plan and regularly check in to see if it needs to be adjusted to fit your family's needs. They'll also help you navigate the legal changes you'll face once your children turn 18, create healthcare directives that will help your children navigate the changes they'll face as *you* grow older, and get your kids started on the right track to preserving their own legacies.

But not all families grow the same way. Some take on new branches, adding stepparents, stepchildren, or children from previous relationships along the way. Estate planning in these situations requires even more care and clarity. Just ask the Targaryens. If *Game of Thrones* teaches us anything, it's that complex family dynamics can bring love, conflict, and sometimes legal gray areas that need to be considered carefully. In the next chapter, we'll look at how to create a plan that supports everyone involved—clearly, fairly, and with care.

Chapter 4

Heirs of Fire and Friction— Navigating Complex Family Dynamics

---

The only thing that could tear down the House of
the Dragon was itself.

–Princess Rhaenyra, *House of the Dragon*

Watching *House of the Dragon* can feel like taking a crash course in advanced genealogy. By the second episode, you're not just asking "who's that?" You're asking "wait, whose child is that person, exactly?" The show's tangled web of marriages, half-siblings, and whispered parentage makes for great television, but in the real world, it's a recipe for legal headaches. Even if you're not a *Game of Thrones* fan, you probably know that the show's family dynamics are more than just chaotic: they make up a cluttered mess that requires reams of paper to navigate (not to mention the number of sponges and mops it would take to clean up all that blood!).

When family trees grow in complicated directions, deciding who inherits what isn't just about fairness. It's about preventing the kind of succession battles that create gripping drama but make real life miserable. A striking example of this kind of tangled succession (and the real consequences it can bring) comes straight from the Targaryen dynasty in *House of the Dragon.*

Before he died, King Viserys Targaryen trained his daughter, Rhaenyra, in the arts of statecraft and included her in the Small Council meetings. Eventually, he named her his heir, and lords and knights supported his decision. But after Viserys died, Ser Otto, the Hand of the King (essentially his successor trustee), argued that Prince Aegon the Elder (the son Viserys had with his second wife, Queen Alicent) should inherit the throne instead. I'm sure the fact that Queen Alicent was Ser Otto's daughter played no role in his decision. This conflict sparked the "Dance of the Dragons"—a war that totally devastated the Targaryens and dragons alike.

When you stop and think about it, one of the things that makes *House of the Dragon* so compelling is that every character believes they're doing the right thing for their family. Rhaenyra believes she's protecting her rightful inheritance. Otto thinks he's securing his and his grandchildren's future. The problem is that by "doing the right thing for their family," at least one of them is going against Viserys' wishes and doing the wrong thing for the ones Viserys wanted to provide for.

Fortunately for most of us, having a "complex family dynamic" usually refers to stepfamilies and blended families rather than bloody weddings and dynastic wars. Essentially, the term "complex family" really boils down to a family that is a mixture of more than one "traditional family unit" (father, mother, and children). A complex family can be as simple as a single parent who shares a child with a former partner who is now in another relationship, or as intricate as the *Game of Thrones* family trees.

While I won't be able to cover every type of complex family in this chapter (I'm not sure I could do that in an entire book, to be honest), I'll show you some of the most common issues complex families face. Maybe you're part of a complex family, or perhaps you've never considered the possibility that a complex family might be in your partner's future if you're no longer here. Either way, this chapter will help you explore the possibilities for the kinds of situations that can, and often do, arise when life doesn't go exactly according to plan.

Complex Families Are the New Normal

First, let's talk about the fact that complex families are indeed the new normal. As Bobby Singer points out in the television show *Supernatural*, "Family don't end with blood." According to Bobby, it doesn't start there either. Bobby helped raise Dean and Sam, and for him, "family" is defined by love and being there for each other, not by DNA. In the episode "No Rest for the Wicked," before Dean and Sam can sneak off and leave him behind as they begin their search for the demon Lilith, Bobby steals the distributor cap from Dean's Impala and tells them he's coming along, whether they like it or not. Fortunately, most complex families don't build bonds by slaying demons and fighting the forces of evil. Instead, as Dean says in a later episode, "Family cares about you. Not what you can do for them. Family is there for the good, bad, all of it. They got your back, even when it hurts. That's family."

Currently in the US, a large number of families are built through bonds of love rather than DNA. According to the US Census Bureau, in 2021, over 20% of couples who lived together at the time of data collection had children from multiple partners.[24] Furthermore, the percentage of children living in a married (first marriage), two-parent household changed from 77% in 1980 to 64.5% in 2022.[25] That means if you're reading this book, there's a really good chance your family doesn't look like the Cleavers from *Leave It to Beaver*. And that's perfectly normal. But it does mean your efforts in estate planning need to be much more thoughtful than Ward Cleaver's ever were.

People have different feelings about these changes. Some celebrate the flexibility and choice modern families represent, while others value the stability and commitment they associate with traditional family structures. Regardless of your personal beliefs about how families should be formed, the reality is that today's families come in configurations that previous generations rarely experienced. And those differences create estate planning challenges that didn't exist when most families followed a single, predictable pattern.

We often think of complex families as simple adjustments to the number or identity of parents within a given household. Two parents divorce, marry other people, and boom! Complex family. Or as we see with *The Brady Bunch*, two parents die, the other two parents marry each other, and boom! Another

---

24 Brittany King and Tayelor Valero, "Over One in Five Couples Who Live Together Have Children from Multiple Partners," Census.gov, August 1, 2023, https://www.census.gov/library/stories/2023/08/multiple-partners-multiple-children.html.

25 https://www.statista.com/statistics/458023/percentage-of-children-in-the-us-by-family-structure/.

complex family. But let's not overlook the fact that parents don't have to be married to be stepparents.

If *The Brady Bunch* were remade today, we might see this scenario: Mike and Carol aren't married but live together as domestic partners, two of Mike's three sons have a different mother than the third, Carol and Mike have a child together, and Carol's sister replaces Alice (the live-in housekeeper) as the third adult in the home. Halfway through the second season, Mike's mother moves in, changing the dynamic to a multigenerational household. In the third season, we might even see Mike's mother marry Sam the butcher and move into the family's newly converted garage apartment.

Navigating this increasingly intricate familial landscape is tricky enough when you're just planning dinner; it becomes even more complicated when inheritance comes into play. And before you say that you don't think your spouse would ever get remarried after you pass, remember that they don't have to be married to be in a complex family. Plus, you can't expect them to mimic *Downton Abbey's* Violet Crawley and remain loyal to you until their own death.

Part of me wants to think that if I go first, my husband will never remarry. But he's such a catch! He cooks, fixes cars, and knows martial arts—plus a million and one survival tricks. He's just a really reliable, all-around consistent, solid guy. He's the guy you'd choose first to be on your zombie apocalypse survival team. He says he won't get remarried, but I know that there will be a lot of women after him. And as long as they wait until I'm gone, I'm fine with that.

I know that no one wants to think about their partner remarrying or "moving on" after they die, but it's a circumstance worth considering. Develop a plan that recognizes the different paths your surviving partner may choose after you're gone and clearly articulates how your legacy, both emotional and material, should be honored, regardless of the choices they make in a future without you in it. Let's look into some of the things you can do to ensure your plan is as clear and precise as it needs to be.

Avoid Cliffhangers—Say What You Mean in Your Plan

Estate planning isn't something you want to improvise. Whether you're part of a complex family, expect to become part of one, or think being part of one could never happen to you, being intentional about your plan now means your deepest wishes for your loved ones will be honored, even as your family's story continues to unfold.

In *House of the Dragon*, one of the most heartbreaking and frustrating moments in the first season is King Viserys's deathbed scene. His wishes for succession were misunderstood, leading to chaos and bloodshed. Viserys believed everything would work out fine, but he *could* have done much more to ensure his intentions were clear and legally binding. Let's break down where Viserys went wrong:

- **Lack of Clear Communication:** Viserys couldn't make up his mind regarding the matter of succession. He named his daughter Rhaenyra as his heir but failed to consistently reinforce this decision—especially after the birth of his sons by his second wife, Alicent Hightower.

- **Mixed Messages:** On Viserys's deathbed, his vague and confusing words to Alicent about Aegon were misinterpreted. This miscommunication directly resulted from his failure to have these crucial conversations and documents formally clarified and witnessed.

- **Failure to Address Competing Claims:** By not making a definitive and public declaration that could have helped his plan avoid disputes, Viserys allowed factions to form around both Rhaenyra and Aegon II, leading to the brutal civil war known as the Dance of the Dragons.

- **Lack of Legal Binding Documents:** Viserys did not ensure his wishes were legally binding and therefore indisputable. Instead, he relied too much on verbal declarations without taking the time to create the necessary documentation that would allow his succession plans to be easily enforced.

Kings aren't the only people who need to use this level of specificity when creating their estate plans. We regular folks need to clearly identify and document our wishes if we want them to be carried out by those we leave behind.

A colleague once shared a story with me about a client who had remarried after his wife passed and, according to his first wife's wishes, was continuing to support his college-aged daughter through school. Regrettably, he became incapacitated, and his new wife decided she no longer wanted to support her stepdaughter and canceled those payments, which created a hardship for the daughter. Since his first wife had no estate plan and he failed to establish a legal obligation for the continued support of their daughter, his second wife was well within her rights to end it, regardless of whether you agree with her decision.

That poor daughter. Not only did she lose her mom, but now the promise her mom made to see her through college is gone too. The man's second wife isn't evil; she's just prioritizing her own family. But that doesn't make the daughter any less financially screwed or emotionally devastated.

Many people don't realize that you have choices about how your assets are handled when you're gone. If you don't have an estate plan, your spouse will most likely inherit everything and then have to make decisions about what, if anything, your children will receive—often while they're still grieving and possibly under pressure from others in their life.

Many loving couples hesitate to include specific provisions about what will happen to their assets if they are the first spouse to pass because it feels as though they're questioning their partner's love or judgment. But here's what I've learned from years of helping families: this isn't about trust—it's about clarity. When you create thoughtful guidelines, you remove the burden of guessing about what you would have wanted and protect your spouse from having to make tough decisions that others might question or resent.

It's like this: if your spouse has 100% control over what you want your child to inherit (such as funds from your insurance policy), and it winds up in a shared account with their new partner, what's to keep that new partner from accessing it to buy a new truck or invest in the latest form of bitcoin?

One way to avoid this type of drama is to appoint an independent trustee who can oversee how your assets are allocated. Doing so will ensure that your child's future is protected. Imagine this: your partner's new spouse's ex, with whom they share a child, wants access to your child's inheritance because it's "only fair that all of the kids be treated equally." (OK, that was a little too much like that moment in *Spaceballs* when Dark Helmet tells Lone Starr, "I am your father's brother's nephew's cousin's former roommate," but you get the idea.) An independent trustee can keep that money out of the hands of an ex-spouse or other people who should have no say in the choices that have to do with your legacy.

If you don't feel comfortable including an independent trustee in general, you can structure your estate plan so that if your spouse remarries, an independent trustee will take control of your children's inheritance—unless the new spouse agrees to a prenuptial agreement that protects those assets. This will give your surviving spouse choices while ensuring your children's inheritance is protected from anyone who might want to use that inheritance to support their own story.

Failing to Plan Lets Others Rewrite Your Family's Future

If there's one thing I've learned since I became a lawyer, it's that we all have different dreams for how we want to live our lives, and that's beautiful. Some families prioritize creating memories through regular vacations over building college savings. Others pour their hearts into planning the wedding of their dreams, finding joy in driving a car that makes them smile every morning, or investing in themselves in ways that make them feel confident and happy.

There's nothing wrong with any of these choices. We all get to decide what brings meaning to our lives. But if you want to ensure that your children's inheritance is used in ways that align with *your* values and dreams for their future instead of someone else's, then you need a clear estate plan that reflects those priorities.

Here's where things can get even more complex. When families blend together, love multiplies—but so do the emotional dynamics that can influence financial decisions. Understandably, people are likely to prioritize their biological children over their stepchildren, even if they love their stepchildren very much. One of the most common (and seemingly harmless) ways this happens is when the stepparent wants to "make things fair" because their biological children don't have the same resources or opportunities that their stepchild does.

For example, if your parents are still alive and dote on your biological child but not your child's stepsiblings, their stepparent might ask for funds from your child's inheritance to make things "fair" for their children. If your spouse has 100% control over your estate, they may very well give in to their new partner's request, which will drain the funds you've left for your child's future.

In some cases, parents of complex families decide to designate multiple trustees, typically one child from each side of the family, so it looks like they're being "fair" and not favoring one child over another. They believe they're setting up a situation where there's equitable control over the family's assets. But there's a big problem with this option: it sets those children up for potential conflict in the future.

Picture this: John and Tim, now co-trustees, disagree about how to handle their younger sibling's college fund. John thinks private school is essential; Tim believes community college plus trade school makes more sense. What started as an attempt to be fair has now put your children in an impossible position: they're forced to argue with each other about decisions you could have made clear from the beginning. Worse yet, if they can't reach an agreement, they may end up in court, watching legal fees drain away the very inheritance they're fighting to protect.

But perhaps the most emotionally complex scenario I've witnessed involves something no family ever wants to face: serious illness. As everyone knows, medical care in the US is expensive, and severe illnesses, such as cancer, can bankrupt a family regardless of who falls victim to them. But when it's a child who's sick, things become even more complicated. Let's say that you've left a $5 million life insurance policy to your child, and their future stepsibling is diagnosed with leukemia. Your child's new stepparent begs your surviving spouse to help with the mounting bills. Who would want to say no to that? It's especially difficult if, like many stepparents, your former partner has come to love their new stepchild.

No one who doesn't live in a secret lair and twirl their mustache while maniacally cackling at the suffering of others wants to see a child suffer while their family struggles to keep their home.

Here's where thoughtful planning becomes an act of love for everyone involved. When you've created specific guidelines for how and when your child's inheritance can be used, you're actually protecting your surviving spouse from ever being placed in such an emotionally devastating position. Instead of having to choose between helping a sick child and honoring your wishes, they can simply say, "I wish I could help, but the trust won't allow it."

Your clear planning doesn't just protect your child's inheritance; it protects your spouse's heart. It removes them from having to be the "bad guy" who says no to a desperate family in crisis because the decision has already been made with wisdom and foresight rather than in the midst of emotional turmoil.

Fortunately, your partner is unlikely to experience such an awful situation. Instead, they're more likely to be asked to help fund things like their stepchildren's education. If you've spent any time on Reddit, you've seen tons of stories about stepparents attempting to appropriate their stepchild's inheritance for their own biological child's education. For example, one Redditor, u/Latter_Pudding_9938, asked, "AITA for not letting my inheritance be used for my step and half-siblings when I'm not going to college?"[26] Essentially, Latter_

---

26 U/Latter_Pudding_9938, "AITA for not letting my inheritance be used for my step and half siblings when I'm not going to college?" Reddit, 2023, https://www.reddit.com/r/AmItheAsshole/comments/1g86wxd/aita_for_not_letting_my_inheritance_be_used_for/.

Pudding_9938 decided he wanted to go to a trade school rather than college.

While his mother accepted his decision, she and his stepfather suggested that he give his inheritance to his stepbrother and half-siblings so they could pay for college and repay him later. She even told him that his deceased father would want him to give them the money. She used a dead man's hypothetical wishes to guilt her own son into giving away his inheritance from his father. And the worst part? She probably genuinely believes it's the right thing to do. When he asked if she really thought his father would want him to give his inheritance to "random kids who aren't me," she said they weren't random to her, so yes, his deceased father would want that. Clearly, she loves her biological children and stepchildren and is doing her best to help them. And who can fault her, really? Other than Latter_Pudding_9938, that is.

Another Redditor, u/country819, asked, "AITA for Not Sharing My Inheritance with My Step-Siblings?"[27] Unlike the previous example, country819 was 30 when he received a substantial inheritance from his grandfather. His stepsiblings, who weren't biologically related to his grandfather, weren't included in the will. His stepmother gently suggested that "sharing some of the inheritance with them would be the fair thing to do, considering we are family." She mentioned it could help with their student loans and starting their careers. (There's that "fair" thing again.) Country819 refused, stating that this inheritance was his grandfather's way of looking out for him. However,

---

27 U/country819, "AITA for Not Sharing My Inheritance with My Step-Siblings?" Reddit, 2023, https://www.reddit.com/r/AITAH/comments/18mvxcc/aita_for_not_sharing_my_inheritance_with_my/?utm_source=chatgpt.com.

some of his friends sided with his stepmother and said he was being selfish and should have shared it because they were family, even though he was never close with his stepsiblings. One reply to his post hits the nail on the head: "This isn't an oops I forgot to send a birthday card, this was an intentional choice [the grandfather] made."[28]

Money isn't the only type of inheritance you want to protect. Consider a story posted by Redditor u/Whention4548 on the r/AITA subreddit.[29] His wife passed away and willed a ring, a family heirloom, to her only child, and she wanted the ring to be given to her daughter when the daughter turned 18. But his new wife wanted him to give the ring to *her* biological daughter to show the new wife's daughter that he loved her just as much as *his* biological daughter. This ring had been passed down through the women in his first wife's family for multiple generations, and his new wife wanted him to break that tradition on a whim. If he agreed to her wishes, his daughter would have been forever separated from the rich family history bound to that ring.

I have to wonder if Cinderella's father would have given a family heirloom like that to one of his stepdaughters. Given the way Cinderella's stepmother manipulated him into believing she would be a good mother to Cinderella, I'd have to say that he probably would. Cinderella's story could easily have been

---

28 U/Eve-3, reply to U/country 819, Reddit, 2023, https://www.reddit.com/r/AITAH/comments/18mvxcc/aita_for_not_sharing_my_inheritance_with_my/?utm_source=chatgpt.com.

29 U/Whention4548, "WIBTA if I give a family heirloom belonging to my late wife to my adopted daughter?" Reddit, 2022, https://www.reddit.com/r/AmItheAsshole/comments/vvym1j/wibta_if_i_give_a_family_heirloom_belonging_to_my/?utm_source=share&utm_medium=android_app&utm_name=androidcss&utm_term=1&utm_content=share_button.

prevented if her father had designated guardians to care for her after his passing. He loved his new wife; why would he worry about whether she would take care of his only child? Of course she would! Or would she?

Fairy tales aren't just stories for children. If you read them closely enough, you'll see they have lessons for adults in them too. Hansel and Gretel? Talk to your kids about taking food from strangers. Sleeping Beauty? Don't snub the powerful aunt who can make your life miserable. Cinderella? Write a solid estate plan to protect your kids. And Snow White? Sometimes, family isn't defined by blood. Sometimes, it's the people you find along the way.

Planning for the Family You Find Along the Way

In *Guardians of the Galaxy, Volume 2*, Yondu (a Ravager with a mystical mohawk) saves Peter Quill from Peter's biological father, Ego (who just happens to be a primordial being with nearly ultimate power). Yondu tells Peter that Ego may have been his father, "but he wasn't your daddy." Yondu raised and cared for Peter and (spoiler alert) ultimately sacrificed himself to save Peter's life. Yondu was Peter's daddy, and Peter was what we might call a "child of Yondu's heart."

Such children may not be biologically related to us, and they may be living happy lives with their parents, but they're still ours in a way. We're the honorary aunties and uncles they turn to when their parents just don't get them. Maybe you're the one who taught them to drive stick shift, or you're the adult they text when they're experiencing their first heartbreak. Or you're the person who shows up to every single one of their school plays, even when their own grandparents can't be bothered. We help shape the lives of these "children of the heart" in countless ways. And we may even be first on their parents' list of guardians in their own estate plans.

Just like biological children, they can greatly benefit from the things we leave behind, whether it be insurance policies, books, clothes, or anything else that is meaningful and reminds them of who you were together. While these relationships don't always have a legal definition, they matter to you, and they're worth protecting.

Of course, our "children of the heart" aren't the only family we've found along the way. Today's families often include arrangements that don't have automatic legal recognition. Close friends who share households and responsibilities, multigenerational living situations, people in polyamorous relationships, and other family structures matter deeply to the people involved, but not to the state.

These relationships create meaningful bonds and responsibilities, but they often lack the legal protections that automatically come with marriage or blood relations. In the next chapter, I'll identify some of the estate planning challenges these arrangements can create and show you how to ensure that the people who matter to you are protected, regardless of how your family is structured.

Chapter 5

#FoundFamily—Planning for the Heroes of Unconventional Households

---

We are Groot.

–Groot, *Guardians of the Galaxy*

The other Airbenders may be gone, but you still have a family. Sokka and I, we're your family now.

–Katara, *Avatar: The Last Airbender*

In the last chapter, we talked about Yondu and Peter Quill and the way they functioned as a found family, but it wasn't just the two of them who ended up in that type of family. Rocket and Groot were already living life supporting each other (AKA platonic life partners) when they were paired with Peter Quill, Gamora, and Drax. By the end of the movie, they were part of a big (slightly dysfunctional) found family that was able to band together to save the universe.

And, like the Guardians, one thing I absolutely love about nerd culture is how accepting everyone is. We all know what it's like to be an outcast. We're the kid no one wanted to sit with at lunch because we couldn't stop talking about Pokémon or Naruto, or we're the adult who excitedly gushes over the latest Marvel movie trailer while everyone else just stares.

Personally, the year *Mass Effect 2* was released, I couldn't hold a conversation without mentioning it, no matter who I was talking to. (I'm sure anyone who knew me in 2012 remembers this phase too.) We've all been the "too much" person in a room full of people who didn't get us before.

I also adore the fact that nearly every fandom centers around narratives of inclusion and acceptance while underscoring (or even fighting against) those who seek to exclude or control others.

Our position as social outcasts has led many of us to find and create our own families—ones that love and accept us just as we are. Perhaps that's the reason behind the rising popularity of the "Found Family" trope in recent popular culture. Do a quick search for #FoundFamily and #ChosenFamily on X (formerly Twitter), Reddit, or Archive of Our Own, and you'll find thousands of stories (both real and fictional) that illustrate just how important found families are to people like you and me.

One of the most popular representations of found families is in *Avatar: The Last Airbender*. At the heart of the series is Fire Lord Ozai, who wants to dominate the world by any means necessary, including unfortunate tactics like genocide and mass murder. As the Avatar (a being who can bend all four elements), Aang is a critical obstacle to Ozai's goal, so Ozai sends his son, Prince Zuko, to capture Aang so that Aang can then be imprisoned forever.

As the story progresses, we see Aang (the last airbender), Katara (a waterbender), her brother Sokka, and Toph (an earthbender) form an unlikely family (known by fans as the Gaang). Together, they help Aang figure out his destiny and stay out of Fire Lord Ozai's grasp. Over time, Zuko understands the damage his father's quest for world domination has caused, and he turns his back on Ozai and, along with his Uncle Iroh, joins Aang and the others.

These wildly disparate characters bond over shared experiences and values to create the family that each of them previously lacked for one reason or another. Similar found families appear in nearly every fandom and genre—think *The Lord of the Rings: The Fellowship of the Ring* (fantasy), *Firefly* and *Serenity* (sci-fi), *Haikyu!!* (manga/anime), and *Parks and Recreation* (mockumentary). These narratives are so appealing because they show us that the adage "you can't choose your family" simply isn't true. While we can't choose the people we're biologically related to, we can create a new family made up of the people we love.

In some cases, we build found families because we're alone in a new place. In other cases, like the one with Prince Zuko, we realize that our values no longer match those of our parents. And, unfortunately for some of us, we build new families because the ones we were born into tell us we're no longer welcome.

So, we create spaces like Comic-Cons and anime conventions where we're welcome and where we welcome others. Don't believe me? Simply go to a Comic-Con and people-watch. In the line to enter the building, you'll see people in basic T-shirts and jeans, superhero costumes, fursuits, and ornate cosplay that must have taken months to create. You might even see my favorite: people who've found ways to create unimaginable crossover outfits such as Iron Man Buzz Lightyear, *Scooby-Doo*'s Daphne as a Ghostbuster, and Snow White/Boba Fett—a crossover aptly titled "Snowba Fett."[30] And everyone walks through the crowd as if they belong there…because they do.

We're nerds. We love different. We *are* different.

And because we celebrate what makes us unique, many of us find ourselves in relationships that don't fit the traditional norm—unmarried and cohabiting, platonic partnerships, polyamorous arrangements, and countless other beautiful ways humans choose to build families together. (There are so many ways to love and create family that I couldn't possibly cover them all in this chapter, let alone the entire book, so if your relationship style isn't mentioned here, please know it's not because I don't see you.)

Chosen family isn't defined by shared bloodlines or marriage certificates. It's defined by commitment and care and who shows up when life gets hard. They're the people who bring you soup when you're sick, who celebrate your weird victories, and who know exactly what to say when your world falls apart.

---

30 Eva, "Top 10 AU and Crossover Cosplays," Geek Chic Elite, January 30, 2015, https://www.geekchicelite.com/top-10-au-crossover-cosplays/.

Chosen family is made up of the people who see all of you and *choose* to stay, day after day.

While the limitless variety of relationships my fellow nerds enter into is astoundingly awesome, the hard truth is that there's an automatic legal protection that comes with a marriage license or blood relation. A legally recognized spouse will typically inherit some or all of their partner's estate, even without an estate plan (though it'll be after probate takes a chunk out of it). And most often, they will be the one who makes healthcare decisions when the other spouse is incapacitated. If you don't have a legal document that says, "this person (or group of people) has the right to make X decisions about my health and estate," the ones you love typically won't have a say in those decisions. They'll be made by someone the court chooses, and the appointed person's decisions won't always align with your values.

So, the person who knows you want *Firefly* playing in the background if you're ever in a coma? Legally irrelevant. The person who's been splitting rent with you for eight years and knows exactly how you want your comic collection handled? They won't have a say. And your partner, who knows if you want to remain on life support? No standing whatsoever. They'd experience the same barriers faced by LGBTQIA+ couples prior to the legalization of gay marriage.

No Paper, No Rights: The Real-Life Stakes of Being Legally Invisible

Until the Supreme Court's 2015 decision legalizing gay marriage, states had the power to decide whether same-sex marriages would be legally recognized. This meant that in many states, people in LGBTQIA+ partnerships had no legal authority to care for their spouses.

Take Sharon Kowalski's story, for example.[31] She and her wife, Karen Thompson, moved in together in 1979, exchanged rings in a marriage ceremony, and were listed as beneficiaries on each other's insurance policies. For all intents and purposes, they were married. But they were women, so according to the state they lived in, they weren't.

In 1983, Sharon was hit by a drunk driver, and the car accident left her with a traumatic brain injury and severe disabilities. Karen petitioned for guardianship of her now-incapacitated wife, but Sharon's father filed and won a counter-petition.

When Sharon's father became too ill to care for her, Karen again petitioned to serve as her wife's guardian. Sharon's doctors supported the request, noting that Sharon clearly expressed her wish to return home with Karen and that this arrangement was in her best interests. Nevertheless, Sharon's family opposed the petition and urged the court to appoint a "neutral" guardian—a Kowalski family friend instead.

Even though neither the family friend nor the Kowalskis were willing to care for her full-time in their homes (which meant that Sharon would need to be institutionalized), the family friend was given guardianship of Kowalski in April 1991.

---

31 *In re Guardianship of Kowalski*, No. C2-91-1047, 478 N.W.2d 790 (1991) (Minnesota Ct. App. Feb. 10, 1991). https://law.justia.com/cases/minnesota/court-of-appeals/1991/c2-91-1047.html.

Karen eventually won by appeal, and her wife Sharon was able to return home in December 1991, eight years after her accident.

Eight years. All because they didn't have a piece of paper that said, "Karen has the right to make legal and medical decisions on Sharon's behalf." Eight years of Sharon's life were stolen not by the drunk driver, but by a legal system that refused to recognize the woman who loved her most. Eight years of Karen fighting just for the right to care for the person she'd already been caring for. All because love without legal documentation is invisible to the law.

I'm not just referring to nontraditional and LGBTQIA+ relationships here. Non-married couples in traditionally recognized romantic relationships (i.e., male and female) don't fare much better than couples like Sharon Kowalski and Karen Thompson when it comes to estates, inheritances, and advanced healthcare directives (medical power of attorney). Too many people believe the myth that merely being in a long-term relationship or living with their partner means they will be considered common-law married and have the same rights as married couples. But no matter what pop culture tells you, they won't.

Unmarried and Legally Unrecognized: The Common-Law Marriage Myth

As much as I love pop culture, it can definitely be a source of misinformation. Case in point? Common-law marriage. Thanks to TV and movies, such as *The Seven Year Hitch*, countless people believe that if they live with a member of the opposite sex for a set amount of time (typically seven years), they'll automatically be married. Therefore, they won't need that piece of paper.

This myth is so dangerous. You're building a life with someone—maybe caring for their aging parents, buying a home together, and planning your futures around each other— and the whole time, you think you're legally protected when you're actually completely vulnerable. As a lawyer, this kind of thing just boggles my mind. I mean, if just living with someone for seven years means you'll automatically inherit everything they have, you need to shop around for wealthier roommates.

Seriously, though, if something is said often and with authority, people will believe it.

Here's a question I often ask clients in nontraditional relationships: how long does it take to be legally recognized as being in a common-law marriage in California? Can you guess their answer? Yup, they say seven years. Every time.

But they're wrong.

You see, there is no common-law marriage in California. As of 2025, common-law marriage is only recognized in the District of Columbia and ten states: Alabama, Colorado, Iowa, Kansas, Montana, Oklahoma, Rhode Island, South Carolina, Utah (by court petition), and Texas. And as was true for gay marriage before 2015, a state that doesn't allow for common-law marriage doesn't have to accept the validity of a common-law marriage from another state. Therefore, if you have a common-law marriage in Texas and move to Florida, you may not have legal spousal rights to shared assets if your partner passes or have a say in the medical care of your partner if they become incapacitated.

In the states that *do* recognize common-law marriages, simply living together for any length of time doesn't mean the state will recognize a couple as anything other than roommates. The couple needs to live together, agree that they're married, plan to get legally married, and present themselves as a married couple in public (using the same last name, sharing bank accounts and property, identifying each other as spouses, and so on). There's no magic amount of time that instantly switches you from roomies to married.

People also believe that sharing a home and having a child together means they're common-law married. This is even scarier, to be honest. Firstly, having a child together is as effective as simply living together—doing so won't magically establish shared possessions or a medical power of attorney. And secondly, having a child means that there's someone else who isn't covered by a nonexistent estate plan.

The misconception that is most worrying is the belief that cohabiting couples or domestic partners have the same rights as married couples. As Sharon Kowalski's story sadly illustrates, you can scream that you're married until you're blue in the face, but if you don't have something with the equivalent of a government stamp on it, you won't have the same rights as married couples.

For example, in Alaska, a man and a woman were domestic partners for 20 years. When he died without a will, she filed a claim against the estate, but the courts denied her because Alaska's succession laws don't recognize domestic partnerships.[32] So much for seven years, right?

In this case, an estate plan that named the surviving partner as the beneficiary would have helped by leaps and bounds. She wouldn't have been left without access to her share of the property and assets that were in her partner's name alone, and his promise to "provide for her for the rest of her life" would have been fulfilled.

Even worse, without an estate plan, your partner could be left with no say in what happens to your remains. Do you want to be buried or cremated? Do you want to donate your body to science? Do you want your loved ones to be able to say goodbye at a funeral service and grieve for you as they need to? If so, you need to plan for those things.

This scenario isn't too dissimilar from what Wanda experienced in Episode 8 of *WandaVision*.[33] When Vision died, all Wanda wanted to do was bury his remains and say goodbye. But she didn't have the right to do so. When she tells acting director Hayward that she's Vision's next of kin and that he is all she has, Hayward replies, "Well, that's just it, Wanda. He isn't yours. He's ours." While we can understand why Hayward sees Vision as $3 billion worth of vibranium, we can also understand that to Wanda he's her soulmate, and she deserves the right to inter Vision's remains according to their joint wishes.

---

32 *In re Estate of Hatten*, No. S-16402, 449 P.3D 256 (2019) https://alr.law.duke.edu/2020/04/in-re-estate-of-hatten/.

33 *WandaVision*, episode 8, "Previously On," directed by Matt Shakman, Written by Laura Donney, Jac Schaeffer, and Peter Cameron, Featuring Elizabeth Olsen and Josh Stamberg, aired February 26, 2021, on Disney Plus.

If you think this is only something that can happen in a fictional world like the MCU, I invite you to think about what this might look like in real life. A colleague recently told me about a client who died in a car accident. Sadly, he didn't realize that his estranged mother had authority over his remains, and she withheld information about his funeral from his partner and their two children. His partner called the local mortuary, but she was told that his mother refused permission to share that information. As a result, his family wasn't able to say their final goodbyes.

Many people in long-term relationships expect to be recognized as their partner's next of kin. But as we've seen, living together and loving each other doesn't make for a legally-binding relationship, especially if the state considers you to be nothing more than roommates.

Roomies, Responsibility, and Real Life

It's interesting that while our culture privileges the nuclear family structure, it also predominantly refuses to accept the validity of these families if the adults involved haven't paid for documentation that essentially says, "Yup! You're a family now." As we've seen, domestic partners in decades-long committed relationships don't have the same benefits as a couple who has been married for two weeks.

But what happens if the people in the household aren't in a domestic partnership? What happens if deep bonds of friendship (and maybe a little bit of a biological relationship) are the foundation of the household structure? How can familial and platonic households avoid the difficulties that can arise when a member of the family unit dies or is incapacitated?

In *The Golden Girls*, when Blanche Devereaux posted an ad for roommates on the grocery store bulletin board, she wasn't expecting to sow the seeds for a new type of family. But early in the series, she, Rose, Dorothy, and Sophia formed close-knit bonds that can only be described as just that: family.

Thinking back on that show, I have to wonder if Blanche ever put the other women on the title of her house, or if any of them revised their estate plans to provide for the others upon their passing or incapacity. For example, would Blanche and Rose continue to support Sophia in Dorothy's absence, or would she be sent back to Shady Pines? If Rose experienced the same type of car accident as Sharon Kowalski, would the other women be able to care for her, or would Rose's children take her back to Minnesota (or wherever they were living at the time)? Would the women even be able to make interim medical decisions after such an accident until Rose's children could be contacted?

Can you imagine Dorothy in a hospital waiting room, being told she has no right to information about Rose's condition because she's "just a roommate?" Ooh! The earful she'd have given the doctor who told her that would have been so spicy! I can even envision the finger pointing and the death stare she'd be leveling the whole time. But regardless of how angrily or eloquently she challenged the medical staff, she still wouldn't know what was going on because technically, she wasn't family.

These women shared everything: meals, secrets, late-night cheesecake therapy sessions. But in the eyes of the law, they'd be strangers.

Sure, you're not going to add every roommate you will ever have to your estate plan. That would be chaotic, and let's be honest, most of the time a roommate is just a roommate. You may be friends, but you're not necessarily family. I'm talking about the people who are there for you when the rain starts to pour and will still be there for you like they've been there before, because you're there for them too. (I'm so sorry for putting that song in your head. I couldn't help myself.)

These households can become pretty complicated. Yours might include you, your child from a previous relationship, their closest cousin, their cousin's child, and your best friend. If yours is the only name on the house's title, who would get the house when you leave this world? If your child is a minor, they won't be able to access it immediately. If you're not married to your romantic partner, they won't necessarily get it either. Who would the state choose to inherit your home (or receive funds from the sale of it)? Where would the rest of your homegrown family live? Would they start fighting with each other over who should be able to stay in the home or who should be named the new owner?

And if these questions aren't complicated enough, consider this one: what happens when multiple adults in the household are romantically involved with each other? While roommates may face legal obstacles, people in multi-partner families often face social biases that limit their rights in unforeseen (and sometimes unseen) ways.

More Than a Pair: Protecting Multi-Partner Families

Just like LGBTQIA+ couples prior to the legalization of gay marriage, multi-partner families often lack the automatic legal protections that come with traditional marriage or blood relations. These families come in many forms—some include multiple adults in romantic relationships with each other, while others may contain a blend of romantic and aromantic relationships in ways that work beautifully for the people involved.

For example, imagine a family of three loving adults: Riley, Jordan, and Chris. While Chris and Jordan are legally married, Riley is just as much of a loving partner as they are. However, because the state only recognizes legally married *couples*, Riley wouldn't have the right to make medical decisions for Chris or Jordan, even if Riley is a registered nurse and is the better choice to do so. Without proper legal documentation, the people who know and love you the most might be legally powerless to help when you need them.

You might be tempted to say, "If something happens to Chris, Jordan can make decisions for them." Okay, but what if *both* Chris and Jordan are in a car accident and are incapacitated? Or what if something happens to Riley? Neither Chris nor Jordan would be able to make medical, financial, or any other type of decision for them. (As we'll see in chapter 8, a good estate planning lawyer will ask questions like this so that they can help you build a comprehensive plan to cover every contingency.)

Social and cultural biases can further complicate the abilities of multi-partner families to care for each other. If anything, the Sharon Kowalski case illustrates how courts can be influenced by personal biases. The appeals court noted that the original ruling favored the Kowalskis because the court agreed with their disapproval of the openness of Sharon and Karen's relationship and the fact that Sharon took Karen to LGBTQIA+ events. While the appeals court didn't explicitly state that bias affected the original ruling, the implication was there.[34]

Multi-partner families need strong, well-crafted legal documents that can withstand potential challenges and provide protection during vulnerable moments. While the law may be written in black and white, courts are made up of people, and people bring their own perspectives to legal decisions. Clear documentation helps ensure your chosen family won't face additional obstacles due to unfamiliarity with how your household works—or skepticism about unconventional family structures.

The beautiful thing about chosen family is that it's intentional. You've already done the hard work of deciding who belongs in your inner circle. Now, you just need to ensure that the law recognizes those deliberate, loving choices.

And speaking of society making assumptions about who deserves legal protection—let's talk about another group that gets the same dismissive treatment: people whose life stories don't include children, whether they wrote that plotline

---

34 *In re Guardianship of Kowalski*, No. C2-91-1047, 478 N.W.2d 790 (1991) (Minnesota Ct. App. Feb. 10, 1991). https://law.justia.com/cases/minnesota/court-of-appeals/1991/c2-91-1047.html.

intentionally, were handed a completely different script than they expected, or are still in the middle of their story not knowing how it will end.

Being childfree doesn't mean you don't have anyone or anything to protect, nor does it mean your estate plan should be an afterthought. The questions simply change. Not only are there people (and pets) you love and want to care for, but your collections, your legacy, and your story also need to be protected and preserved. We'll talk about what that looks like next.

Chapter 6

With Great Power Comes Great Legacy—Defining Your Legacy on Your Own Terms

Life isn't just about passing on your genes. We can leave behind much more than just DNA. Through speech, music, literature and movies...what we've seen, heard, felt...anger, joy and sorrow...these are the things I will pass on.

–Solid Snake, *Metal Gear Solid 2: Sons of Liberty*

Maybe sometime after you crossed into your 30s, you suddenly realized...you're not the young, untested protagonist anymore.

You've graduated. Leveled up. You're the godparent. The dog mom. The cool aunt or uncle who knows the best late-night food spots, gives the most thoughtful birthday gifts, and always seems to know *exactly* what to say when things fall apart.

You're Sokka, post-Gaang, with the war behind you and perspective ahead. Older, wiser, and a little less sarcastic—but still the one people count on to ground them when everything else feels too big.

You're Hagrid. Not the headmaster. Not the chosen one. But the heart. The one who made all the difference by *being there*— loyal, generous, and larger than life.

You're the character people wish had their own spinoff or prequel. Your story is interesting in unexpected ways, and your experiences vary from the norm. Because of this, you're the adult who remembers what it felt like to be misunderstood, so you make sure the next generation knows they're not alone.

You're not lost, you're *seasoned*. You're not settling, you're *choosing*. And if you don't have kids of your own, maybe the people around you act like you're missing a step, like your story hasn't "fully begun."

And maybe, just maybe, you're Uncle Ben and Aunt May—the ones who didn't get their own superhero origin story, but who *created* one for someone else. Peter Parker's greatest power didn't come from a radioactive spider bite. It came from two people who had no obligation to love him, but chose to anyway. Two people who poured their values, their wisdom, and their unwavering support into a kid who wasn't "theirs," but became theirs by choice.

Uncle Ben and Aunt May never wore capes or saved the world directly. But their legacy? Their legacy literally saved the world over and over again. Like Solid Snake, they passed on something far more important than DNA to Peter. Every time Spider-Man chose to fight the bad guys or help the people of New York instead of walk away, every time he remembered that Uncle Ben had said "with great power comes great responsibility," he lived out the values they instilled in him.

Peter Parker could save the world because two people chose to love a kid who wasn't theirs. They didn't need to see him become Spider-Man to know their love mattered. They just loved him fully and completely, and that love changed everything.

That's the thing about being childfree that the world often misses: you don't need to create life to create a legacy. Sometimes the most powerful legacies come from the people who had the space, the resources, and the open hearts to pour everything they had into shaping the future through the lives they chose to touch.

Whether you're fiercely independent or devoted to a life partner (with or without a legal title), you know that building a meaningful life isn't defined by the number of tiny humans you get to raise. You've built your life around shared experiences, chosen family, sacred solitude, or an unshakable partnership that doesn't need a label.

Some of us deliberately chart a path without children, making conscious decisions that align with our values and vision for life. Others may have hoped for children but found life had different plans. Whether you're childfree by choice or by circumstance, your story still matters deeply.

If no one has ever told you this: you don't need to be a parent to have a powerful legacy.

Your legacy lives in how you show up, the friends you never abandoned, the causes you championed, and the way you made your own rules while making room for others.

But that freedom comes with responsibility. When you don't have kids automatically inheriting everything, every choice becomes intentional. Every decision about where your story goes next is yours to make. That's both terrifying and incredibly powerful. Your values, your stories, your care…all of them can be passed down to the people, causes, and communities that matter most to *you*.

Because your life is wide open, your legacy can be as unique, strange, generous, and epic as you are. But that also means you have to plan for it intentionally. If you don't decide where your story goes once you're gone, *someone else will*.

This chapter is for you: the child-free heroes, the wanderers, the mentors, the fierce weirdos, and those who make their own paths. You may not have kids, but you're raising the future in your own way. And it's time to protect that.

Let's make your legacy legendary.

It's the Story You Leave Behind

On the surface, the word "legacy" is traditionally tied to the money and tangible items we leave behind. But it's so much more than that. It's all of the parts of you—what you've seen, heard, and felt—that make up the story of who you are, and they're the things your loved ones will value the most.

When most people think of estate planning, they picture legal documents like wills, trusts, and powers of attorney. And yes, those things are important, but true legacy planning is about much more than paperwork.

I recently came across a story that beautifully illustrates this. Hideo Kojima is one of the most influential video game creators in the world known for titles like *Metal Gear Solid* and *Death Stranding*, which have been played by millions of people worldwide. But even if you've never touched a video game, his recent actions offer an important lesson that gives us new ways to approach how we prepare for the future.

During the pandemic, Kojima fell seriously ill—an experience that forced him to confront a difficult question many of us prefer to avoid: how much time do I have left?

Rather than ignore that question, he made a deeply intentional choice. He entrusted his assistant with a USB drive containing all of his personal creative ideas—essentially a blueprint his team could use to continue his work if he were no longer able to. Through this act, Kojima created something incredibly meaningful: an ethical will.

While a will handles your financial and legal affairs (who inherits your assets, how property is distributed, and who manages your estate), an ethical will (sometimes called a legacy letter or values statement) passes on something different: your values, wisdom, personal story, and the lessons you want your loved ones to carry forward. An ethical will doesn't just preserve your story; it enables you to pass on your lived experiences.

Equippable by Others? Inventory Management IRL

The things we leave behind also tell the story of who we are. As childfree adults who typically have disposable income that parents would spend on their children (and if you're in a dual income household, you're even more likely to have some spare cash), it's pretty easy to build an extensive collection of valuable items that we care deeply about. When you consider that many of us are kids with adult money (we are finally able to buy the expensive and cool toys we really wanted as kids), it's no wonder that the collectible industry is huge.

From Funko Pop! to Amiibo figurines and from comic books to pristine, never-opened Star Wars action figures, we have a lot of stuff. And some of that stuff is pretty valuable. Most of us are aware that mint condition comic books and in-the-box toys regularly appreciate in value. (If you're like me, you've listened in horror to stories about that one guy whose mom threw out all of his boxed Star Wars action figures or left his comics in a damp basement only for them to be covered in mildew.) Did you know that your Pokémon cards, LEGO™ sets, and even some of your Funko Pop! figures can also appreciate in value? In 2001, I spent $100 on a LEGO Star Wars TIE Fighter set for my husband—today, it's worth over $1,000.

The one-of-a-kind collectibles many of us own are on a whole other level. Consider the hefty price tags on anime collectibles, for example. There's the Hatsune Miku 15th Anniversary figure valued at over $1,000, the Super Sonico Jumbo Poly figure valued at $2,000, the Life-sized Momo Belia Deviluke bridal version for $27,000, and the very shiny 24 karat gold RX-78-2 Gundam at $200,000.[35]

While I certainly don't have the bank balance to be able to shell out thousands of dollars on collectibles (hey, just because I'm a lawyer doesn't mean I have a ton of cash—I do live in California after all!), I'm not immune to their pull. I recently acquired an adorable Cardcaptor Sakura Banpresto figure at Anime Expo for just $30.

The Good Smile Company makes gorgeous Cardcaptor Sakura figures that run for hundreds of dollars. I look at their Always Together ~Pinky Promise~ figure created for CLAMP's 30th anniversary every now and then and fantasize about where I'd put her.[36] Honestly, I remember when I first saw her debut at Anime Expo, and it felt like one of those '80s movies where everything moves in slow motion. But for now, being able to place my Banpresto on my desk in front of a journal with an embossed Cardcaptor magic seal makes me happy.

When I'm gone, I want to know that she's going to continue to be cared for. That doesn't mean that my husband needs to keep her. He's more of a Star Wars guy anyway. But it does mean that I want her to go to someone I love, or at least be sold for a fair value. The last thing I want is for her to be listed on Facebook Marketplace and sold for $3.50 or tossed in a donation bin somewhere.

It might sound silly to read that a plastic figurine makes me happy, but she represents so much to me. She's worth far more than the $30 I spent. Every time I see her, the joy of finding her and the memories of that convention come back to me. Since she appears behind me whenever I have a Zoom call, I feel those emotions practically every day. She's a small piece of my story, and I want my story to be treated with care.

At one L.A. Comic Con I attended, I spoke to someone whose uncle was a huge Star Trek fan and collected tons of memorabilia. When he died, he had no estate plan, so the memorabilia has been sitting in a garage for two years because his sister didn't know what to do with it. Imagine that: a lifetime of passion, carefully curated pieces that brought him joy, now gathering dust because no one understood what those items meant to him or what he would want them to do with his collectibles. His sister isn't heartless; she just doesn't know the difference between a mass-produced toy and a rare collectible. Without guidance, a collection that could honor his memory or bring joy to other fans is just becoming junk.

One year, a fellow Comic-Con attendee approached my booth and said he didn't need an estate plan because his wife was going to send his $100,000 worth of collectibles to the auction house. That's great and all, but how long will it take her to get paid if he hasn't already inventoried his items and had them professionally appraised? Unfortunately, he left quickly before I could even ask this one question.

The auction house isn't going to rush his collection through appraisals just because his wife needs the money right now. In fact, unappraised items will be at the bottom of their to-do list because they'll prioritize items ready for immediate sale. And don't forget that they're not going to be able to sell everything in one fell swoop. Most likely, they'll sell a little bit here and a little bit there. If that $100,000 is a substitute or supplement to his life insurance, it's likely she'll struggle to stay afloat until the auction house has the chance to go through everything. So unless she's willing to let them buy the entire lot of his collection at once, she won't see that money for a long time. If she does let them buy it all at once, she's going to take a huge loss since it's not appraised.

Part of developing a solid estate plan involves sorting out your inventory and deciding what can be donated, what can be sold and for how much, and what should be passed on to someone else. It's like going to a vendor in a video game. Most of them have a "sell all junk" option that lets you quickly cash in on items that have little or no value to you (your socks, for example) and a "sell" option that allows you to sell items for a price you approve (if you don't like the price, you don't sell). Or, you can open your pack and ask your friends if they need or want some of your gear. Without an estate plan, your friends and family are left to sort through your treasures, and if they don't know any better, they might just click "sell all junk" and call it a day.

And Your Little Dog, Too

Fortunately, when you die in a video game, you don't have to worry about what will happen to your character's pets. They'll simply respawn alongside you when you return to your last save. It's too bad life doesn't have a similar save feature.

When planning for your pet, you might be tempted to write in your will, "I leave all my possessions to my dog, Toto." After all, he's your fur baby. Why wouldn't you want him to have the best of everything once you're gone? He's the one who greets you after every terrible day, knows when you need extra snuggles, and has been your constant companion through moves, breakups, career changes, and everything else life has thrown at you. But while you may think of Toto as a person (he's the only one who *truly* gets you, after all), the state sees him as a possession, and possessions can't inherit your things.

You're probably thinking, "Fine. I'll leave my money to my bestie so she can take care of Toto." But wills don't work that way. When you leave money to someone in a will with verbal instructions about pet care, those instructions are legally meaningless. Your best friend could love Toto with all her heart and genuinely intend to follow your wishes, but when her transmission fails or she faces a medical emergency, there's nothing in place to stop her from using "Toto's money" for her own needs.

She's not being malicious; she's being human. She's staring at a $3,000 car repair bill, knowing she can't get to work without her car, and there's this money sitting in her account. She tells herself she'll pay it back when things get better. But life keeps happening, and suddenly "Toto's money" is gone, and your beloved companion is eating the cheapest food possible or going without important medication while your friend struggles with guilt.

Here's the bottom line: the law sees it as her money, period. Sure, she might feel guilty about it, but guilt doesn't pay for premium dog food or emergency vet bills.

And just like choosing a guardian for human children, you want to make sure you name more than one potential guardian for your pet. What if your best friend's daughter develops an allergy to Toto? What's plan B?

This doesn't mean that you can't take care of your pets once you're gone. You just need to make sure you do it the right way, and that's by creating a pet trust.

The beauty of a pet trust is that it creates legally enforceable obligations. The money you set aside can *only* be used for your pet's care; it's not a gift to the caregiver that comes with a hopeful suggestion. (You can definitely leave them a separate gift as a thank you for taking Toto in, though.) Essentially, a pet trust names a guardian (or a list of guardians) who will care for your pet if you die or are incapacitated. It enables the guardian to access funds to care for your pet and allows you to stipulate how your pet is to be cared for. You can specify everything from basic preventative care (such as flea and heartworm treatments, regular grooming appointments, dental cleanings, and shots) to managing chronic health issues (such as diabetes, kidney disease, and even cancer).

Pet trusts aren't uncommon. All 50 states recognize the validity of pet trusts (that's five times more than the number of states that recognize common-law marriage!). Even Majel Roddenberry, the wife of Star Trek creator Gene Roddenberry, established a trust for their dogs that provided $4 million for their care, which included a stipulation that they remain in the family home for the rest of their lives and granted $1 million to the dogs' new guardian.[37]

An essential part of any trust, including pet trusts, is the appointment of a trustee, and it's a good idea to appoint someone other than your pet's new guardian. This creates a system of checks and balances and names someone whose job it is to ensure the money actually goes to Toto's care, not to car repairs. Otherwise, we're back to your friend's transmission failing and the funds you've set aside for Toto going to the mechanic. After all, who's going to report it?

Fund Your Own Wayne Foundation

Maybe you've decided to include a pet trust in your estate plan, ensuring your furry companions have the care they deserve after you're gone. That alone is a powerful legacy. But even if you're not a pet person, you can still create an amazing plan.

Take a moment to consider the things you care about the most. This can include causes you care about and have championed throughout your life, as well as the places and activities you enjoy. Which of them could use your support?

For example, if you're an avid video gamer, you might want to donate some of your assets to organizations like Child's Play Charity, which brings gaming into children's hospital rooms (you can donate money, games, and equipment)[38] or

---

37 Andrew Greiner, "'Star Trek' Fortune Goes to the Dogs," NBC Miami, April 23, 2009, https://www.nbcmiami.com/news/weird/roddenberry-fortune-goes-to-the-dogs/1859600/.

38 https://www.childsplaycharity.org/.

AbleGamers, which uses video games to improve the quality of life for people with disabilities.[39]

Perhaps you're an anime fan. If your life has been impacted in some way by a mental illness and you want to give others access to the resources you had (or wish you had), consider working with an organization like Anime for Humanity, which works to end the stigmas surrounding mental health.[40]

If you're someone who finds meaning at the intersection of faith and fandom, you might consider donating some of your assets to an organization like mine, Jesus Otaku, which is an anime-based ministry dedicated to sharing one simple, life-changing truth with fellow nerds: God loves you exactly as you are.[41] Other incredible organizations in this space include Love Thy Nerd,[42] which explores how our favorite stories connect to faith and life, and GameChurch,[43] which builds community around gaming and spiritual growth. These ministries understand that sacred and nerdy aren't mutually exclusive; they're beautifully complementary.

Is your Han Solo in carbonite figure still in its original packaging? Do you have a ton of Star Wars memorabilia on your shelves or in boxes in your attic? Consider reaching out to your fellow Star Wars fans at Rancho Obi-Wan,[44] a nonprofit museum that holds the world's largest Star Wars memorabilia

39 https://ablegamers.org/.
40 https://animeforhumanity.org/.
41 https://www.jesusotaku.com/.
42 https://lovethynerd.com/.
43 https://gamechurch.com/.
44 https://ranchoobiwan.org/.

collection, and ask how you can share your own collection with current and future fans.

Real-life comic book superheroes would also welcome your help. The Hero Initiative provides emergency medical and financial support to comic creators who are often on the brink of bankruptcy.[45] If you're concerned about comic book preservation, you might want to support the Golden Apple Comic & Art Foundation, a nonprofit whose goal is to "preserve, safeguard, and showcase" comics.[46]

And don't forget about all the tangible things you create (we'll talk about digital creations in the next section). Do you love crafting? Do you knit, paint, or make cosplay costumes? Plenty of organizations will happily accept your supplies (and some will even take your creations) and use them to help the next generation of crafters design new things to share with the world.

Most of us care about so many things at once that it's nearly impossible to name them in the spur of the moment. That's one of the reasons I conduct legacy interviews: simple, guided conversations where my clients share their personal stories, values, and life lessons.

It's during these interviews that many of my clients realize what's really important to them. For example, one client recalled that as a child, she spent a great deal of time at the public library, which intensely benefited her life. So she decided to donate to the public library because she wanted to ensure

---

45 https://www.heroinitiative.org/.
46 https://goldenapplecomics.com/pages/charity?srsltid=AfmBOooVgGV6RISiJ-LO8f5F
  b3KxO4JLxoLtXvVdA4K_6m5A_6X01HCM

that it would still be there to help other kids in the future the way it helped her.

Giving to charity doesn't require that you give a lot, and in some cases, it doesn't even involve giving money. It's all a matter of supporting the things you care about in a way that works best for you, even if all you do is donate your suits to Dress for Success[47] or your art supplies to the local elementary school. Unlike a simple will, which can be conveniently "lost" by someone who either wants to sell your belongings or can't be bothered to donate them, spelling out your wishes in a comprehensive estate plan will ensure your desires are met and the people and groups you want to support receive what you've left for them.

Curate Your Digital Archive

Our digital creations and possessions are just as important as our physical ones. We create YouTube videos, TikToks, blogs, fan fiction, digital art, social media stories, games, and apps at an astounding rate, but no one will keep them alive after we're gone unless we set things in motion now. We're the first generation to have a significant digital life, and it's important to understand that if we want to preserve our presence in cyberspace after we're gone, we need to plan for that too.

Like I mentioned before, Hideo Kojima saved his ideas on a USB drive, which is fine, but what's to keep that USB drive from winding up in someone's desk drawer for years? A better way to keep your digital legacy alive is by using digital archives. They allow you to share your ideas with your family or the

---

47 https://dressforsuccess.org/.

world, and your estate plan can ensure those archives remain accessible for generations to come. Take one of my clients, for example. He's a musician and hosts his music on a website. Part of his estate plan includes a trust that has funds to pay for the website's hosting fees.

If you're looking for a place to preserve your library of videos, TikToks, music, art, or other digital intellectual property, websites such as Culture Hive[48] and Artwork Archive[49] are great places to start. Just don't forget to consider who you'll grant access to your creations. For example, you can make your creations free to use or charge licensing fees to help cover hosting and maintenance costs. If that seems complicated, don't worry. The archive you decide to work with will be able to help you make the choices that best fit your preferences.

Some museums will also preserve your digital legacy. You've probably heard about the National Archives[50] and the Library of Congress,[51] but there are museums dedicated to nerd and geek culture that will ensure that the stories you create will live on long after you do. Archive of Our Own (AO3)[52] preserves fan fiction, while Rhizome,[53] located at the New Museum in New York City, supports and preserves new media art. You can store your digital items on Google Drive and then set up a Google Inactive Account Manager so that the account doesn't get deleted due to inactivity. That way you can store

---

48 https://www.culturehive.co.uk/digital-heritage-hub/resource/content/creating-digital-archive/.

49 https://www.artworkarchive.com/.

50 https://www.archives.gov/.

51 https://www.loc.gov/.

52 https://archiveofourown.org/.

53 https://rhizome.org/.

and share many of your creations on Google Drive and provide continued access to your digital creations for years to come.

Don't forget about the intangible things you own. They're also a large part of who you are and are worth preserving and sharing, if possible. You've spent years building your game library. But here's the uncomfortable truth most gamers don't realize: you don't actually own most of those games.

If you're anything like me, you're fed up with the growing trend toward digital and subscription-based ownership. If I buy a copy of *Fallout 4*, I want to literally own a copy of *Fallout 4*. I don't want to own a nontransferable code for the game on Steam. In many cases, you're simply renting access under complex licensing agreements.

Just look at what happened when Crunchyroll acquired Funimation.[54] They completely eliminated the Funimation platform entirely, and people who had purchased digital videos lost access to content they thought they owned. Years of digital purchases were suddenly gone. While Crunchyroll is considering providing discounts on their subscription services or giving users a rebate for the amount it would cost to access those videos from another platform, these "solutions" are more of a quick fix than anything long-lasting. Users will be faced with giving up the videos they love for a few dollars or accessing them on another platform that could then take the same path as Crunchyroll.

---

54 Isiah Colbert, "Crunchyroll President Responds to Concerns Over Lost Digital Copies Due to Funimation Merger," IGN, March 7, 2024, https://www.ign.com/articles/crunchyroll-president-responds-to-concerns-over-lost-digital-copies-due-to-funimation-merger/.

When you're gone, or even before that, your digital legacy could also disappear overnight.

Enter GOG (Good Old Games). As reported by PC Gamer, GOG made headlines by officially allowing gamers to pass on their Digital Rights Management-free (DRM-free) libraries to heirs as long as they're properly documented through their estate plan.[55] That means you can pass *The Witcher 3: Wild Hunt* to your sibling, leave *Cyberpunk 2077: Ultimate Edition* to your best friend, and hand down your DRM-free collection of *Baldur's Gate 3*, *Disco Elysium*, and *Divinity: Original Sin 2* to the next generation. Most importantly, it means that your hard-earned collection on GOG won't just disappear.

GOG is one of the few platforms that gives gamers a real path to preserve their digital legacy. But sadly, they're still the exception. Most platforms profit by keeping full control of games, blocking their transfers, and forcing new game purchases.

This is where we come in. Millennials and Gen X are the first digital-native generations facing these legacy questions head-on. Our digital lives matter regardless of whether they're preserved in photos, crypto, online accounts, or our gaming libraries. We have collective power here. If we really want to see change, we have to speak up and demand it by contacting platforms directly, supporting companies like GOG, and making our opinions known through our purchasing decisions. The more we educate ourselves, ask hard questions,

---

55 Andy Chalk, "GOG Will Let You Bequeath Your Game Library to Someone Else as Long as You Can Prove You're Actually Dead," *PCGamer*, June 6, 2024, https://www.pcgamer.com/gaming-industry/gog-will-let-you-bequeath-your-game-library-to-someone-else-as-long-as-you-can-prove-youre-actually-dead/.

and refuse to accept "that's just how it works," the more likely we are to force real change to happen.

Until then, I tell everyone three essential steps for protecting digital assets. First, set up a password manager that allows you to name an emergency contact. Second, if you have a Google account, set up the Inactive Account Manager. Third, if you use Apple, set up a Legacy Contact. These aren't perfect solutions, but they're the foundation of any digital legacy plan.

As you create an inventory of the physical things you'll leave behind, also create a digital inventory. Make secure lists of your accounts (Nintendo, Steam, GOG, PlayStation, Xbox, Mojang, etc.), including usernames, passwords, backup codes, and two-factor authentication (2FA) details. Store them securely in a password manager or digital vault service that allows your loved ones (biological and otherwise) to access your information after your passing.

Digital assets might seem like a small detail, but they highlight just how complicated estate planning can be. And when things get this complex, shortcuts (like trying to DIY your plan) can end up causing more harm than good. With that in mind, let's look at why trying to handle your estate plan on your own is a recipe for disaster.

Chapter 7

Don't Choose Your Own Adventure—Why a DIY Estate Plan Will Not Turn Out How You Expect

This is what I wanted...and this is what I got.

—r/ExpectationVsReality

Have you ever watched someone make or build something and thought to yourself, "That's simple. I could do that!"?

When a pro does a job, it *should* look easy. They're a *pro*. It's what they do. It's what they've spent years training and thousands of dollars to learn how to do. For example, someone who builds houses has spent years building the muscle memory it takes to lay just the right amount of grout for bathroom tiles, memorized the best ways to hang a cabinet, and studied how to install complex electrical systems without zapping themselves into the great beyond.

You'll turn on a DIY show and watch a pro painter effortlessly paint a wall in a matter of minutes, cutting in the corners without a thought for painter's tape, and you suddenly want to paint your own bedroom. It's like those Choose Your Own Adventure books. "Do you want to hire a professional painter (turn to page 47) or tackle this yourself (turn to page 23)?"

Maybe you turn to page 23, head to Lowe's, grab some paint and brushes, and come home giddy with excitement. An hour later, there's paint dribbled on the floor because you forgot to buy a drop cloth, and the makeshift cardboard floor protection you created from old Amazon boxes keeps slipping out of place. And there's paint smeared in several places on the once pristine white ceiling because you tried to cut in the corners without painter's tape (just like the pro did on TV). Now, you're exhausted, your back hurts, and you still have three and a half walls left to do. And as you climb down from the far-too-short ladder, you notice that you forgot to remove the face plates from the electrical outlets, so they're smeared with paint as well.

A few days later, you've made at least two more trips to Lowe's for additional supplies: another gallon of paint because you didn't buy enough the first time, a can of white paint to touch up the ceiling, new faceplates for the outlets, and other items you should have bought the first time around. That's when you suddenly realize that the color you chose is far too dark for your space, and you feel like you've painted yourself into a tomb.

As you stand there comparing the picture-perfect room of your dreams on your phone screen to the slightly uneven paint job and the mess of brushes, rollers, buckets, and paint-smeared Amazon boxes you now need to clean up, you realize you're in over your head. As you hold up the photo of your dream room and look around the disaster area you've created, it's clear that you're the living embodiment of the "this is what I wanted vs. this is what I got" meme that was all the rage in 2021. (My favorite versions of that meme are the baking ones where someone tries to recreate a cute photo of a gingerbread man cookie holding a candy cane, only to end up with mutant blobs that look like they came straight out of a *Resident Evil* movie.)

It's the real-world version of turning to page 23 in your adventure book only to read: "You have made a terrible mistake. Your quest ends in disaster. Try again."

But hey, at least you saved a few bucks, right?

Well, if you were to buy the cheapest versions of everything you need (not counting a good ladder) at Lowe's, you'd spend around $600. The average cost of hiring a professional painter to paint a bedroom can range from around $400 to $1,000, depending on the size of the room and the complexity of the project.

If you type "what do I need to paint a room" into Google, you'll quickly get a list of the different tools and cans of paint you'd need to refresh a room and even some how-to videos. But when you factor in the Tylenol for your sore muscles, the stress of messing something up only to do it again, the time spent painting, going back and forth to Lowe's, and cleaning up the mess, the high end of that range starts to sound like a good deal.

Once you've painted one room, you'll have a better understanding of what you need to do to make the process go smoothly the next time. Practice and experience, after all, are what make someone a pro. But, and I'm not throwing shade at painters here, estate planning is more complex than house painting. If you do a search for "what do I need to create an estate plan," you'll find the results are far more complex than a list of painting supplies and a couple of videos.

Plenty of books and websites will tell you that it's simple and that all you need to do is answer a few questions, and you'll be good to go. It's even easier than painting a room! But the truth is that DIY-ing your estate plan can cause problems that are far worse than sore muscles and spilled paint. While it may feel like you're saving money by going it alone, in the long run, that couldn't be further from the truth.

You Get What You Pay For

I get it. Money is tight, the rent is too high, and when your kid needs braces or your car needs new brakes, an estate plan probably won't be high on your to-do list. Given the cost of living today, there's no question as to why people would turn to a free online will planning site to just get the job done and off their to-do list.

But the simplicity and "budget-friendly" nature of online will planning sites is, in the words of our favorite Mon Calamari, Admiral Ackbar, "a trap." In *Return of the Jedi*, all the rebels needed to do was take a quick trip to Endor, disable the Death Star's shields, and wait for the fleet to do its job. Sure, things turned out fine in the end, but I can't help but feel bad for all of the little Ewoks who got blasted into oblivion.

And while Luke Skywalker was able to step in at the last minute and save the day, the same can't be said about your will. It's your *last will and testament*. In other words, it's the *last* version of the document. Once you're gone, there's no revising it. If you've gone with the Temu or Ali Express version of estate planning, well, you get what you pay for.

Unlike Choose Your Own Adventure books, you can't flip the pages and find a better ending.

One low-cost legal document site will sell you a will for the low, low price of $99! It includes the will, a healthcare directive, financial power of attorney, HIPAA authorization, 30 days of free revisions, and printing and shipping of one set of documents. You can pay them $99, fill out your own documents, and have them do absolutely nothing else to help you.

But wait! There's more! For only $249, a real attorney will review your documents, and you also receive unlimited 30-minute calls with *some* attorney for a whole year! Sure, you won't always get the same attorney each time you call, or even an attorney from the same firm as the last one, but at least there's an attorney associated with your will. (Don't forget that you'll also be enrolled in a subscription-based plan that will automatically bill you $199 each year until you cancel. The fine print will get you every time.)

When we were kids, this type of thing would have been advertised in late-night infomercials by someone like Vince, who sold the Slap Chop. Those infomercials might be cringe now, but back then, those infomercials milked millions of dollars out of viewers' pockets. They used tried and true strategies that continue to convince people to pay for ineffective or useless products and services. Among other things, they created a sense of urgency ("Get peace of mind before it's too late!"), focused on the product's benefits ("You'll save money and prepare for your family's future."), and built trust with testimonials ("This site saved me thousands on lawyer fees!") all while hawking a cheaply produced product that would likely sit in the back of your mom's cabinet for the next decade or so.

These simple marketing strategies have worked for generations and will continue to do so for the foreseeable future. The end goal is to sell a one-time product or service and move on to the next customer. It's not to create a relationship or provide real and valuable legal counsel. Free and cheap will websites are traps because they lure you in with the shiny promise of simplicity and leave your loved ones with a complex and often expensive mess when it comes time to deal with your estate.

Take, for example, a thread about DIY wills on the r/Lawyertalk subreddit. One redditor, u/scrapqueen, posted a complaint about DIY wills, venting about a will that was signed by everyone except the person who died, and noted that "it's cheaper to pay for a will than it will be for your heirs to have to fix your screw up!"[56] The majority of the replies share similar stories and frustrations, but the most telling are those by users like u/jjames3213, who stated that "As someone who does estate litigation, nothing I love more than a DIY will," and u/20thCenturyTCK, who simply replied, "Same!" An

---

56 U/scrapqueen, "Another 'do it yourself' will disaster," Reddit, 2024, https://www.reddit.com/r/Lawyertalk/comments/1gxgi36/another_do_it_yourself_will_disaster/.

anonymous user even wrote, "I love people who think lawyers are useless middlemen. They create a lot of good work for me."

Sadly, do-it-yourself legal platforms aren't the only traps that can lead your heirs straight to probate court where litigation attorneys like these three Redditors will take a share of your estate away from your loved ones.

It's Dangerous to Go Alone! Take This!

If you've ever played *The Legend of Zelda*, you know the moment when Link encounters an old man early in the game. If Link interacts with him, the old man gives him a sword to help on his quest to rescue Princess Zelda from her captor, Ganon. Think of the old man as Link's lawyer and his sword as an estate plan. Sure, you can ignore the old man and struggle through battles until you can get a sword on your own, but it won't be easy, and you're likely to die. Many times.

While you won't have to fight your way through countless mobs to DIY your estate plan, going it alone means that your loved ones will face the consequences of your decisions. Even veteran video gamers know to take advantage of power-ups when they're offered; you should do the same.

It's too bad former US Supreme Court Chief Justice Warren E. Burger wasn't a fan of *The Legend of Zelda*. If he had been, perhaps he wouldn't have tried to go it alone when he wrote his will. Sadly, like Chief Justice Burger, many people attempt to DIY their own wills and estate plans, but this approach rarely ends well. If anything, Burger's story illustrates that even *seasoned* lawyers need to consult estate attorneys.

Burger wrote his own will, which was 176 words long, included typos, and cost his heirs $450,000 in taxes (nearly $950,000 today). Although he spent decades learning and interpreting the law, he couldn't see past his own expertise to recognize when he needed help. And worse, because he didn't give his executors the power to sell his real estate. It got tied up in probate, which added legal fees and court costs to the money his estate had to pay. If he'd only spent the estimated $2,000 that an estate planning agency would have charged, his heirs would have received a lot more of his hard-earned legacy.

I get it. In this economy, simply existing is expensive. But as Chief Justice Burger's story illustrates, an estate plan will save your family so much more money in the long run. So, when the credit union or online brokerage firm tells you they can help you do it for only $899, who can blame you for taking them up on their offer? They're professional businesses that handle money; they've got to know what they're doing, right?

Of course they do. They know they're giving you a packet of papers, and you're giving them $899.

When was the last time you bought a car? Was price the only factor in your decision? If you just said, "Yes," you probably bought the cheapest used car you could find, didn't you? How did that work out?

This reminds me of a story my mom once told me that captures why cutting corners on what matters most always backfires. When she first immigrated to the US from the Philippines, she was on a tight budget and scrutinized every expense. Her sister, trying to be helpful, advised her to buy the cheapest car she could find. "Just get something that runs," her sister said, so that's exactly what my mom did.

But before long, she found herself sitting in Los Angeles traffic during a sweltering summer with no air conditioning, cranking down the windows by hand—all while *very* pregnant. I can only imagine how frustrated she must have been: carrying her first child, dealing with morning sickness, and having to wrestle with car windows in the blazing heat simply because she prioritized price over comfort and reliability. (Maybe that's why summer heat is my kryptonite since she was pregnant with *me* at the time, and I was an August baby.)

That story stayed with me because it perfectly captures how "saving money" can end up costing us the things that matter most: comfort, peace of mind, and, in my mom's case, a comfortable pregnancy during LA's brutal summers. Through that experience, she learned that some things are worth investing in properly the first time.

When you buy a cheap car, you end up stuck with the headaches, the breakdowns, and the worries. But with estate planning, when you focus on price instead of protection, and convenience over careful planning, it's your family that truly pays the cost.

The latest shortcut tempting people away from careful estate planning isn't a bargain-bin form. It's artificial intelligence. While AI promises speed, convenience, and seemingly credible information (AI often makes mistakes, but since they're well-written, most people won't recognize them), trusting it with something as high-stakes as your will can be just as risky as the discount templates sold by some websites, only with a shinier interface. And that's what we're going to talk about next.

Sorry, ChatGPT Can't Be Your Lawyer

Recently, a colleague of mine had a couple come in with what looked like an AI-generated will, and it left nothing to the other spouse in the event that one of them died. When this was pointed out to the couple, they were surprised because they thought it was generally assumed. They trusted AI to provide them with expert guidance on this topic, but AI failed to address their most pressing concern. Because lawyers are legally trained, they can spot errors and know which follow-up questions to ask. AI doesn't know, and when it doesn't know something, it hallucinates and creates fake information. When you trust AI, you won't know which questions matter most because AI doesn't push back.

Growing up in the age of both *The Terminator* and *The Matrix*, I'm all too familiar with the speed at which AI can infiltrate human culture. Give us something that will do the heavy lifting for us, and we'll demand that their creators take our money. However, it would be nice if that "heavy lifting" were literal, rather than figurative. Having ChatGPT come and mow the lawn once a week would be wonderful. Well, at least until the robot uprising comes and the lawn mower decides it has had just about enough of me telling it what to do. But what happens when someone asks AI to prepare their loved ones for a future without them?

Since it was first launched in 2022, ChatGPT has quickly become the go-to tool for doing just about anything. Want to bake a cake? Ask ChatGPT for a recipe. Want to tell your kid a bedtime story? Give ChatGPT a basic prompt. Want to write a will? Just write, "I want to write a will. Can you help?" And ChatGPT will give you a template.

It will also state that what it is about to provide you isn't legally binding, that it won't meet state-specific legal requirements, that it's not a substitute for legal advice, and that if there are any mistakes in it, the will can be invalidated by the courts. Unfortunately, most people will just gloss over that information as if it were an iTunes user agreement. (If you haven't seen the episode of *South Park* related to that topic, consider yourself lucky.)

I'm stunned by how many people are likely to turn to AI like ChatGPT, Perplexity, Google Gemini, and others to draft important legal documents. A survey of 4,100 adults in the US and the United Kingdom found that nearly half of them felt comfortable with using AI to write their wills.[57] Their reasoning? AI is cheap and convenient. While cheap and convenient are perfectly fine reasons for choosing where to eat lunch, I'm sure they *aren't* the best reasons for choosing how you communicate your major decisions and preferences about what happens after you die.

Here's the thing about AI: it is incredible at processing information and generating text, but it can't understand the nuances of your family dynamics, your state's specific laws, or the unique challenges your estate might face. It's like asking

---

57 Charlie Coulson, "Would You Allow Artificial Intelligence to Decide What Happens to Everything You Own When You're Gone?" *London Daily News*, July 29, 2025, https://www.londondaily.news/half-of-brits-and-americans-would-trust-ai-to-write-their-will-but-expert-warns-of-serious-risks/.

your GPS to plan your entire life journey—it might get you from point A to point B, but it won't point out the locations that will matter to you along the way.

AI doesn't know that your sister hasn't spoken to your brother in five years, that your daughter struggles with addiction and needs a trust structure to protect her inheritance, or that your son's marriage is rocky and you want to shield his portion from a potential divorce. It doesn't know that your state has specific requirements for witness signatures or that your family business has complexities that require specialized planning. It won't ask about these deeply personal family dynamics that shape your decisions, nor will it guide you through the technical legal requirements that could invalidate your entire plan.

The details that your estate plan entails aren't just legal technicalities. They're specifics about the most important relationships in your life, and they deserve more than algorithmic guesswork. AI is simply generating text based on patterns it's learned rather than providing actual legal counsel tailored to your specific situation and the people you love most.

To top it off, when you ask AI a question about laws and statutes, there's the risk that it might hallucinate. No, seriously. AI hallucinates. All the time. I'm not referring to the same type of hallucinations you might experience on LSD. Rather, when AI hallucinates, it just makes stuff up. (For you younger readers, that's one of the ways your professor knows you didn't write that paper you submitted last week.)

In those Choose Your Own Adventure books, at least the authors had thought through all the possible paths and their consequences and then made concrete connections between them. With AI-generated estate planning, you're essentially writing your own adventure story without knowing where any choices lead while relying on a trail guide using a map from a different country and written in a foreign language.

The Real Adventure: Choosing Professional Guidance

Fortunately, you don't have to guess which path leads to the best outcome in estate planning. With the right guide, you can see the evidence, understand the stakes, and choose the route that actually protects what matters most to you.

The DIY route might seem like the quick, budget-friendly Choose Your Own Adventure plan, but too often it leads to a page that says something like: "Your well-intentioned plan has created chaos for your family and cost them thousands of dollars." The professional path might require a different investment upfront, but it's the route that leads to the ending you actually want.

When choosing legal counsel, the wrong turn can cost a lot more than a few minutes of reading, so it pays to know where your journey should begin, and that's exactly where we're headed next.

Chapter 8

Find the Lawyer You Deserve and the One You Need

He's the hero Gotham deserves, but not the one it needs right now.

—Commissioner Gordon, *The Dark Knight* (2008)

Remember the end of *The Dark Knight*? Commissioner Gordon is standing with his son, explaining why Batman has to take the blame for what Harvey Dent did and then go into hiding. The Commissioner says Batman is "the hero Gotham deserves, but not the one it needs right now." Gordon was talking about how sometimes the right choice isn't the popular choice. Batman was willing to be the villain in everyone's eyes to protect what really mattered—the hope Dent had given the people of Gotham for the future.

Gotham City was full of corrupt cops, lazy bureaucrats, and people who took easy ways out. Sound familiar? Sadly, the legal world has its fair share of those too. But just like Batman refused to accept "good enough" when people's lives were on the line, you shouldn't settle when it comes to protecting your family's legacy.

Because this isn't just about paperwork, it's about the people you love most sleeping soundly at night—knowing they're protected no matter what happens to you.

When it comes to choosing an estate planning attorney, you need that same kind of thinking. Don't go with the lawyer everyone else uses just because they're convenient or the one who quotes you the lowest fees. Don't settle for the one who tells you what you want to hear. You need the one who's actually going to fight for your family's future, even if that means having harder conversations and paying a bit more upfront.

Your family deserves their own Batman—someone who specializes in this stuff, who stays up late learning new ways to protect people, and who's willing to do the difficult work that others won't. Not just whoever happens to be available and is willing to fill out some forms.

Every Hero Needs the Right Partner: How to Find the Alfred to Your Batman and Evade the Red Flags

Whenever we see Batman in The Dark Knight trilogy, he's presented as the lone hero. The singular figure standing against evil. And unlike the comics where he's got the whole Bat-Family backing him up—Robin, Nightwing, Batgirl, Red Hood, and about a dozen other protégés—Christopher Nolan's version of Batman in this trilogy really does seem to be going it alone.

But he's not. He's got something even better than a team of costumed vigilantes: Alfred.

Bruce Wayne may have billions of dollars, and Batman may have countless bat-themed gadgets, but neither of them would be anything without Alfred Pennyworth. To call upon other fandoms: if Batman were James Bond, Alfred would be Q; if Batman were Frodo, Alfred would be Samwise; and if Batman were Neo, Alfred would be Morpheus. Alfred is Batman's guide, mentor, and the person Batman turns to whenever he needs help.

And if Batman were you, Alfred would be your estate planning attorney.

In short, Alfred does everything a good estate planning attorney should do. He knows Bruce's family history better than anyone. He understands what Bruce values most. He's there for the long haul, not just when things are convenient. He gives honest advice even when it's not what Bruce wants to hear. And he's completely devoted to protecting what matters most to the Wayne family legacy.

The trick to finding your own Alfred lies in knowing how to spot red flags so you can avoid trusting someone who will leave you alone and unsupported when the going gets tough.

Red Flag #1: The "I Do Everything" Generalist

One of the most important red flags to watch for is a lawyer who doesn't specialize in estate planning. Choosing the right lawyer is kind of like rolling a character in your favorite tabletop role-playing game or video game. Each character class (fighter, mage, rogue, etc.) relies on specific attributes. For example, fighters need to be strong and have excellent constitutions, mages need to be smart and wise, and rogues need to be intelligent and dexterous. While it might be tempting to spread your points across the board in order to create a "well-rounded" character, doing so will only lead to heartache when you're in the middle of a campaign and realize that your warrior doesn't have enough strength to fight a boss or your mage doesn't have enough spell points to cast high-level spells. It's their specializations that make each character class strong, and the same is true for attorneys.

A lawyer who lists multiple practice areas (such as personal injury, criminal defense, divorce, estate planning, immigration, and corporate law) on their business sign or website has likely spread their skill points too widely to do a truly effective job.

Here's a story that still makes my stomach turn. A colleague of mine once shared office space with a generalist attorney who actually bragged about the profits he was making from estate planning clients. His secret? He got free templates from Rocket Lawyer and sold them for thousands of dollars without any customization for each family's unique situation.

You deserve someone who has chosen to focus their energy specifically on becoming exceptional at protecting families like yours. In some cases, that means working with someone who's further narrowed their focus on a sub-specialization, such as elder care or estate planning for families with special needs children, which is kind of like rolling a mage (a spellcaster who can cast a wide variety of low-level spells) and then further specializing in fire or frost magic (which enables the mage to cast precise and highly-dangerous fire or frost spells).

Do you want to know my specializations? I've basically multiclassed into a Nerd Culture Expert with bonus proficiencies in supporting Young Families and Childfree Adventurers, plus I have a rare achievement unlock for Collectibles and Pop Culture Assets Protection. In other words, I'm an expert in creating guardianship plans and trusts for families with young children, advising childfree adults on how to plan their estates when they don't have direct descendants, and safeguarding treasured collections for collectors—from rare books and fine art to memorabilia and antiques.

In chapter 1, I mentioned that I'm part of a movement of heart-centered estate attorneys called Personal Family Lawyer® or PFL. We're more than just a network—we're attorneys who believe that estate planning should be about relationships, not just transactions. Instead of the traditional "one and done" approach, we focus on becoming trusted advisors who will be there with your family during difficult moments and ensuring that your plan actually works when it matters most.

One thing that sets PFL attorneys apart is our shared commitment to making estate planning our primary focus. We've chosen to center our practices around protecting families and their legacies, rather than generalizing and bouncing between dozens of different legal fields.

Red Flag #2: The Drive-Through Attorney

Because generalists wear so many hats, they don't always have (or make) the time to focus on getting to know their estate planning clients on a personal level. Instead, they serve the fast-food equivalent of an estate plan and try to move their clients through the line as quickly and efficiently as possible. But an estate plan isn't a bag of steaming crispy fries, and it shouldn't be rushed like one.

When you first speak with them (on the phone, online, or in person), they should appear happy to see you and be genuinely interested in what you have to say. This first conversation doesn't necessarily need to be with the attorney—especially if their process includes an in-depth working session later where you'll get substantial time with the lawyer. What matters is that someone takes the time to understand your situation rather than rushing you through a sales pitch.

A good firm will start with a discovery call to answer your questions and help you determine whether their process is a good fit for your family. If a law firm tries to rush through this initial conversation in less than ten minutes or starts throwing out price quotes before they know anything about your family's needs, that's not a good sign.

The actual planning session itself should be comprehensive— we're talking hours, not minutes. And this shouldn't feel like a meet and greet where the attorney is trying to convince you to hire them. This should be a real working session where you're getting customized legal guidance that will guide you through making actual decisions about your family's future.

If you encounter a lawyer who says all this can be done in 30 minutes or less, I urge you to walk away. This is your estate plan, not a Domino's delivery. Your family's future deserves more than fast-food service. When your loved ones are grieving and confused, they'll need documents that are carefully crafted with their specific needs in mind—not something rushed through in the time it takes to grab lunch.

Here's something important that many people don't realize: a good attorney won't just hand you documents and hope you figure out the rest. They should have a process to ensure your documents actually get signed on a specific date rather than leaving it up to chance. You'd be surprised at how many estate plans fail simply because they never get properly signed. People get busy, put it off, and suddenly years have passed with incomplete planning. A good process includes multiple touchpoints from an initial discovery call through a comprehensive planning session, proper document signing, and ongoing maintenance.

But signing the documents is only half the battle. A good estate planning attorney will also give you guidance to help you ensure assets are properly aligned with your new estate plan. This means that your bank accounts, investment accounts, real estate, and other assets are titled correctly to work with your trusts and beneficiary designations. And I'm not talking about a generic set of instructions. This should be personalized guidance based on your specific assets and plans. Many people walk away with beautifully crafted legal documents that don't actually control their assets because this crucial step is often overlooked.

Here's what really sets a good estate planning attorney apart: the relationship doesn't end when the documents are delivered. Your life will change—kids will be born, family members will pass away, laws will evolve, and your financial situation will shift. A good attorney will have some kind of ongoing maintenance process because an estate plan isn't a one and done document; it's a living strategy that needs to grow with your family.

If you contact an attorney and they schedule a ten-minute appointment, or worse, never plan to meet with you at all and instead just have someone fill out forms based on a questionnaire, that's your cue to trust the bad feeling their actions create inside of you. Listen to the Force, and find someone who values you as a person rather than a one-time fee. Don't get me wrong. You'll likely interact with support staff throughout the process, and that's perfectly normal and valuable. What's concerning is when there's no meaningful attorney involvement in your actual planning.

Someone once contacted me about navigating a family member's probate case. When I asked him if he had an estate plan, he described his experience: he contacted a law firm who sent him a questionnaire, and when he returned it, they sent him his documents. There was no significant human interaction with anyone who understood estate planning. He answered some questions, paid $2,500, and got a stack of papers to sign and file away.

That person didn't work with a counselor-at-law; they worked with a robotic document mill in a human suit.

Red Flag #3: The Commission Collector

Speaking of fees, let's be real. As I said in chapter 1, we all know that being a lawyer is a business. Law school costs a fortune, and lawyers have bills to pay just like everyone else. However, if you call a lawyer saying you think you need a trust and they immediately quote you a fee without getting to know you and your specific needs, that's another red flag.

Likewise, if it feels like they're just trying to sell you a product rather than help you understand the process, that may be your sign that they're not the right lawyer for you. It's kind of like going to a personal trainer who, during your first meeting, guarantees that in eight weeks you'll have six-pack abs, and the only way to get there is by using their branded supplements— all without getting to know you or your nutritional and physical needs.

Personally, I'm prediabetic, so sugary protein mixes and bars would be the wrong choice for me. If I went to a personal trainer and they tried to sell me their supplements without even asking one health question, I'd be out of there so fast that I could count "cardio workout" off my to-do list for the day.

Once you know what to look for, red flags like these become easy to spot. Unfortunately, the way lawyers are portrayed in popular culture normalizes problematic behavior to the point that we often fail to recognize it for what it is. I've had many people tell me that the last estate planning attorney they met with just talked *at* them instead of *with* them, and they had no idea what was going on during the entire meeting. They left feeling more confused than when they arrived, with a stack of legal jargon they couldn't understand—and without a clear sense of whether their family was actually protected. Far too often, I see people accept terrible service from their lawyer because Hollywood has convinced us that all attorneys are supposed to be intimidating, condescending jerks who speak in legal jargon and treat clients like nuisances.

While some lawyers do fit this stereotype, the reality is that most lawyers aren't morally corrupt people looking to profit from someone else's misfortune, but many *are* transactional because they haven't been taught any other way to practice estate planning. Many simply aren't trained in estate planning and are doing the best they can with what they know. In fact, the legal profession has reached a point where estate planning is increasingly viewed as a minor concern to the extent that the California Bar Association is considering removing it from the bar exam. This is crazy to me because not everyone will wind up in litigation or in a criminal case during their life, but estate planning is something everyone has to deal with, and they'll need trained and licensed lawyers to help them do it.

Fortunately, if you do a little research and ask the right questions, you can find a good estate planning attorney who understands the importance of the estate planning process and continually works to improve their skills.

XP Isn't Just for Games: Pick a Lawyer Who Regularly Levels Up

One of the things I like about games like *Skyrim* is that there's no real endpoint. As I said in the book's introduction, I hate endings, so games that don't have an absolute end are particularly appealing. Sure, in *Skyrim*, there's the final battle with Alduin, but the game doesn't end there. You can continue leveling your character indefinitely, so there's never a ceiling on progress.

As most gamers know, leveling a character relies on earning experience points (XP) by completing quests and killing enemies and monsters. When you level your character, you get more health and stamina that you need as the enemies get tougher and tougher. Games like *Skyrim* allow you to allocate your XP into categories like archery, lock picking, and magic. But in most games, once you've filled a category, you no longer earn experience when you use that skill. So if you max out your archery tree, killing enemies with your bow does you no good, and you have to use a sword or dagger, which you likely haven't spent any skill points on if you want to get XP from winning the fight. Suddenly, you're facing a level 50 monster with the equivalent of a level 10 sword. Ouch.

Skyrim, however, handles this differently. When you max out a skill, you can reset it to zero. It sounds counterintuitive, but it means you can keep using your preferred weapon, like a bow, to keep earning XP. Better yet, you can reinvest those points into partially developed skills (like swordplay) allowing you to broaden your strengths without abandoning your playstyle.

You want a lawyer who does the same thing. The legal landscape is constantly evolving. New laws, new strategies, and new ways to protect families pop up almost overnight. You want an attorney who's actively leveling up their skills, not someone who learned estate planning once in law school and called it good.

I'm not referring to someone who learns simply for the joy of learning—though I'll admit I'm totally guilty of that. Instead, I'm talking about someone who's always finding new ways to be the best lawyer they can be for their clients by participating in Continuing Legal Education (CLE) courses, attending focused conferences and webinars, and working with their peers to ensure they stay continually up-to-date on all things estate planning. Would you want a doctor who hasn't learned anything new since medical school? Or a financial advisor who wasn't keeping up with changing tax laws? Your family's future deserves the same commitment to staying current.

That's what every PFL attorney does, and it's what makes us stand out among our peers.

We never stop leveling up. We regularly attend estate planning conferences to sharpen our skills, stay current with new developments in the law, and learn from each other's experiences. Think of it like a guild where everyone is committed to becoming the best possible protector of families and their legacies (and some of us actually are the legal equivalent of frost and fire mages, with a few archmages among our ranks).

Sometimes, we form a party together to tackle a more complex situation that needs multiple specialties, which ends up being like a superhero team up. And who doesn't love one of those iconic team up moments or crossover comics?

Generalist lawyers might practice criminal law, civil litigation, drunk driving defense, family law, and possibly a dozen other areas of law in addition to estate planning. They simply won't be able to dedicate as much time to estate planning if they want to stay current on the areas that bring in the most business. That's just Economics 101. But that also means that they won't be as effective when it comes to estate planning because they simply can't invest the time in continuing education about it like we can.

Of course, no amount of education will do you much good if your attorney isn't willing to use it to help you understand the ramifications of the choices you want to make (such as leaving a no-strings-attached million-dollar insurance policy to an 18-year-old or identifying only one guardian for your child). A good estate planning attorney is also a good counselor.

Behind Every Good Plan Is a Good Counselor

Have you ever wondered why lawyers are also called counselors? It's because we're supposed to offer counsel to our clients. Our job is to do more than represent you in a court of law, fight for your innocence, or even make sure your business won't be sued because of a bad product line. Our job is also to be your advisor to help you understand the law so you can make informed decisions about your future.

Thanks to pop culture representations of attorneys, most people don't really understand what an attorney-client relationship should look like—especially when it comes to estate planning. The attorneys we see on TV and in the movies take control of the situation, tell their clients to stay quiet, and make all of the decisions.

True, if you're the defendant in a criminal trial, you want an attorney who can take charge and make strategic decisions to protect you. But estate planning is completely different. You're not in crisis mode. You're making thoughtful decisions about your family's future. In estate planning, you should be in the driver's seat, making the decisions with your attorney as the knowledgeable guide helping you navigate the legal landscape.

You're not hiring someone to fill out forms for you. If that's all you want, don't pay someone to fill in the boxes for you. Just go online and fill them out yourself. No, an actual *counselor-at-law* should be there to help you think through the complex legal, family, and financial decisions you might not have even considered before getting online to make the initial appointment.

In order to be good counselors, we need to get to know you and understand where you're coming from. People will often tell their estate lawyer that they want to set up a trust that will allow their kids to inherit only after they finish college. A lot of lawyers might say, "Sure," and add that requirement. A good lawyer would ask questions like, "What if they decide to go to a trade school? What if they don't finish college? Would the money be forfeited? Are there any other stipulations, such as age, that you would like to consider?"

An estate planning attorney will help you think through family dynamics that could cause problems later. For example, I'd argue against leaving all of your money to one child with the expectation that they'd share it equally with the rest of the children because that's not estate planning—that's wishful thinking. And wishful thinking can tear families apart. They'll also plan for scenarios you haven't considered, like what happens if you've named a couple to be guardians to your kids and then they get divorced. And they'll help you understand asset protection strategies and how to create a plan that will build generational wealth for your family and future generations.

Your lawyer needs to get to know you so they can learn what you don't know. They need to understand not just your assets, but your hopes, your fears, and the unique dynamics that make your family who they are. A good estate planning attorney will get to know you on a personal level because doing so will give them the critical insights that will help them know what questions to ask and which suggestions to make.

A truly exceptional estate planning attorney will be there for you right now and for your family when they need them the most. Because when you're gone, a stack of legal documents can't answer questions, provide guidance, or offer comfort during one of the most difficult times in your family's life. They'll be the steady voice your spouse can call when they're overwhelmed by grief and paperwork. They'll be the person who remembers your wishes when your children are too emotional to think clearly. They'll be your Alfred—the trusted guardian of your family's future.

All of this starts with a conversation, not a group of checklists or a collection of templates. And that conversation should begin from your very first interaction. A good attorney's response to your initial inquiry will give you a preview of how they'll handle your entire matter—either with care and attention or as just another item on their to-do list.

So let's take a look at how that first interaction should go.

Side Quest: The Three Email Challenge

Alright, time to put your money where your mouse is. I've given you all this advice about finding the right attorney, so let's test it out in the real world.

Your mission, should you choose to accept it: send this simple email to three different estate planning attorneys in your area. Think of it as speed dating, but for legal counsel (and with much higher stakes).

Email Template:

Hello [Attorney's Name],

My name is [Your Name], and I'm interested in creating an estate plan for my family. I'd love to learn more about your process and discuss my situation. Could you let me know the best way to get started?

Thank you, [Your Name] [Your Contact Information]

What you're looking for in their responses:

- Professional, timely response vs. no response or days-long delays
- Clear next steps (like informational materials and a way to schedule a call) vs. a vague "we'll get back to you" type of response
- An invitation to have a real conversation vs. immediate price quotes over email
- Organized follow-up process vs. disorganized or confusing communication

The good law firms will want to schedule a call to learn about your situation. That's when you ask the deeper questions about their continuing education, specialization, and approach.

Once you sift through the replies and eliminate the unsatisfactory responses, you can then use the red flags we discussed earlier in this chapter to further narrow your search until you reach the end of your quest for the ultimate prize: an awesome lawyer who will work with you every step of the way.

Plot twist: if you're in California and want to include me in your comparison, just email me and I'll send you my informational materials plus a link to book a discovery call with my office. Or, if you've already decided I'm at the top of your list, just go to my website and book a call directly. Simply visit www.Amo-Law. com, select "Book a Call," and you can pick a time to set up a call. During that call, my team will connect with you, learn about your family and why estate planning is on your mind right now, and help you determine if my approach is the right fit for you. No pressure, no immediate sales pitch—just a real conversation about what matters most to you.

If you're outside California, I can connect you with attorneys in my network who take the same relationship-first approach to estate planning.

But honestly? Even if you don't choose me, this exercise will make you a much smarter consumer of legal services. You'll quickly spot the difference between attorneys who see you as a person and those who see you as a transaction.

Roll the Credits

I hate endings. That's part of the reason why this book is titled *Your After-Credits Scene*, because if something comes after the credits, then the movie isn't over yet.

Fortunately, your movie isn't over yet either. While you don't know how many chapters you have left, you absolutely can control what happens in the scenes that come after you're gone.

We've explored how the stories we love reveal profound truths about protecting the people we care about most. We've learned from Harry Potter that you can't let someone else—even a wise mentor like Dumbledore—make all the crucial decisions for your family. *Game of Thrones* warns us of the conflict that can occur when complex family dynamics aren't properly addressed. *WandaVision* shows us that the deepest, most meaningful relationships can be legally invisible, and those without legal standing need protection most of all. *The Golden Girls* reminds us that family isn't always about blood—sometimes it's about the people who choose to stand by you when everything else falls apart. And we've discovered that whether or not you're a parent, you have people and things worth protecting.

But here's what it all comes down to: the people you love most are counting on you to be their hero today. Not by fighting intergalactic battles or finding the elusive MacGuffin, but by making the simple, thoughtful choice to protect their future.

Your after-credits scene isn't about you. It's about the people you love. It's about your spouse or partner not having to navigate grief and legal confusion alone. It's about your children, chosen family, pets, or the people who depend on you feeling secure in knowing that you thought of everything. It's about ensuring that meaningful relationships, whether recognized by law or not, are protected and honored. It's about your legacy being one of love and protection, not one of stress and uncertainty.

Choose the right guide, write the best ending, and give your family the peace they deserve. Because the greatest superpower of all is knowing that the people you love will be okay—no matter what.

Oh, and if you're ever at the Los Angeles Comic Con, come find my booth and tell me about your favorite fandom! I can't wait to hear all about it!

Here's one last fandom quote for you. My absolute favorite Doctor from the Doctor Who franchise is the Eleventh Doctor. I relate to him because he seems to dislike endings just as much as I do. When he is confronted with the idea that endings are a part of life, he says, "We're all stories in the end, just make it a good one, eh?" And that is my wish for you, to understand that as you build your legacy, your story is one worth telling now and in the future.

Acknowledgments

To Jesus, my Savior and the Author of my story—You knew exactly what You were doing when You made me a lawyer who loves anime, a professional who cosplays, and a woman who finds You in both courtrooms and convention halls. Thank You for showing me that nothing about who I am was accidental. You wove my professional calling and personal passions together for reasons I'm still discovering.

To my husband, Rick—when fear whispered "you can't," your voice was louder, reminding me that dreams don't have expiration dates and the only real failure is never trying at all.

To my sister, Megan—you showed me that being authentic isn't about fitting in, it's about having the courage to stand out. You made weird feel wonderful.

To my parents who sacrificed and worked hard so that I could have amazing opportunities. And modeled what it looked like to be an entrepreneur for me.

To my professional tribe—the attorneys, coaches, and mentors who embraced the whole me and proved that we serve others best when we bring our authentic selves to the work we're called to do.

To every family who trusted me with your most precious concerns—your stories taught me that estate planning isn't really about documents and legal structures. It's about love made tangible and the deep human need to know that what matters most to you will continue to matter.

This book is a testimony to integration—the beautiful process of weaving all the threads of who we are into one authentic tapestry. Legacy, after all, isn't just the money we leave behind. It's the courage to be fully ourselves and the grace to help others do the same.

For we are God's masterpiece. He has created us anew in Christ Jesus, so we can do the good things he planned for us long ago. Ephesians 2:10 (NLT)

About the Author

M. Cecilia Amo, Esq. is an estate planning attorney, pop culture devotee, and unapologetic fandom nerd who's cried over more character deaths than she can count, stayed up way too late binging anime or grinding through video games, and genuinely believes that legacy is more than just the money you leave behind.

As a Xennial who loves both Millennial and Gen X fandoms, Cecilia understands how deeply our generation connects to stories about finding purpose, creating deep bonds, and protecting what matters most. And she believes those same themes deserve just as much attention in real life.

After years in high-stakes litigation and nonprofit leadership, including serving on the board that runs Anime Expo, Cecilia founded AMO LAW Legacy Planning to bring heart-centered, relationship-driven counsel to a space too often defined by impersonal legal forms. Her work transforms estate planning from a dry, transactional task into something more human, intentional, and enduring—a meaningful experience that is grounded in values and love. And in the people who make life worth living.

Her book is an invitation to write your own *after-credits scene—* one where the people you love are cared for. Where your story continues and your legacy lives on.

Because estate planning isn't just about paperwork; it's about crafting a legacy worthy of your own epic hero's journey.